YOU DON'T KNOW MY STORY

trouble

Jennifer Beverly

&

Single Mom Project, LLC

Dedicated to the one I can always rely on and who promised to give double for our troubles. I have the pleasure to humbly serve His Kingdom. He is the Most High whom I give all the glory to.

Citations:

Roberts, Ann. "Are Pisces Women and Libra Man Compatible?" *Love to Know*. Love to Know Corp., 2006-2019, https://horoscopes.lovetoknow.com/Are_Pisces_Wome n_and_Libra_Men_Compatible.

Written By: LEE HUTSON, LEE HUTSON JR., JILL H SCOTT Lyrics © Sony/ATV Music Publishing LLC, Universal Music Publishing Group

Esteban Fernandez, Luricic "Bird Vision Explained". *National Science Foundation. NSF.* 2010. http://estebanfj.bio.purdue.edu/birdvision/visualfields. html

"Bird Brained", Way to Die #378. "Death on a Stick". Aired 8/3/2010. https://1000waystodie.fandom.com/wiki/Bird_Brained

https://www.firstresponse.com/en/Product-Listings/Early-Result-Pregnancy-Test

Do People Actually Tell The Truth When Drunk?. Anaheim Lighthouse. 3/13/2018. https://anaheimlighthouse.com/blog/do-people-actually-tell-the-truth-when-drunk/

ACKNOWLEDGMENTS

Writing a book about my own life is an emotional process. It is harder than I realized yet will be more rewarding than I can every imagine. Although this season of my life was filled with many ups and downs, the downs were not in vain. None of it would have been possible without the help of the relationships God has placed in my life.

To all those that have been a part of me getting there; I am so thankful that words cannot express my gratitude. Truly, I love and appreciate you for your help, support and encouragement: Sam W., Keisha M., and Lauren W. To the sisterhood!

Finally, I thank God for my relationship with Him; pushing me, enlightening me, revealing my purposes, and giving me the resources to finish. Without God, I wouldn't be able to do any of this thing called life.

Author's Note:

Even though tequila with orange wedges is a happy place of mine, I love Jesus even more. (Yes, I said all that in the same sentence.)

When you understand my story, that'll better explain why I love the Lord and am so grateful for Him. Because if it wasn't for Him, I wouldn't be here. Literally.

With that, I'm a woman who knows my strength and help comes from the Lord. It's been written that "trouble produces perseverance, which creates character and then hope", (Romans 5:3-4). So I'm hoping my overall testimony will be relatable, help others and will add to His glory; as I refuse to believe what I've been through has been in vain.

I have chosen (well was forced rather) to grow from the pain, learn from the past, be inspirational, and ultimately be victorious by sharing my story.

So having said all that, have you ever bitten into a grape expecting it to be juicy and sweet but instead, it was surprisingly sour? There is no way of knowing the outcome without actually tasting it yourself. Much like what happened to me, you never know someone until you bite down and realize it's actually sour AF. Get ready to be exposed to my first experiences with Judas, full of eroticism, vulnerability, transparency, and spirituality. What happened? Well... read on my friends. Read on.

XOXO,

Jennifer Beverly

Once upon a time, not long ago...

There was a man and a woman who met at a birthday party. They had instant chemistry, spent a plethora of time together, eventually fell in love, got married, and lived happily ever after.

...SIKE!

(Did I just show my age? Do people even say sike anymore?)

Pisces and Libra as Lovers

(combining an air sign and water sign)

"Pisces is a devoted lover. She wants to please her Libra lover, and he'll let her experiment until her heart's content. Libra adores his mystical Pisces, even though he didn't understand her. He'll do everything humanly possible to assure she's happy. For Pisces, making love is the ultimate expression of her feelings."

Sexual Attraction

"Sexually, these two are compatible. Libra is an attentive lover. Making love is an art form for the Libra male. Pisces turns lovemaking into a mystical, sensual experience. Her love has no limits, and Libra will bask in her adoration."

~Text Message Received~

"Shhh- It's a surprise! Come celebrate Dave's birthday. Since he's never had a surprise birthday party before, it's my duty as his girlfriend to make him feel special.... RSVP yes or no by Wednesday."

Aww, that's sweet, she better let it be known she's the girlfriend, and it's her duty. Lol. Yass!

RSVP: Yes!

I loved that Atlanta Meetup group. There was literally always something to do, and we had so much fun together. Just some young, wild, and free social beings from different walks of life—laughing, partying, and of course, drinking. Just good ass vibes, you know.

For instance, my first Meetup was a few months ago, and the first person I met officially and in person was this down for the cause, natural sista named Shanelle.

Shanelle had a natural black girl puff ponytail, and I found out she was from Charlotte, NC. She was also a Recruiter for a graphic design company. I told her I may know someone looking for a graphic design position, and she gave me her contact info. From there, she gave me the low down on the people and vibes of the group. You know sometimes when you just instantly click with someone? Well, that's how Shanelle and I were.

We quickly meshed, and she introduced me to Penny (or P as most called her). I could tell P was mixed with her thick curly hair, fair skin, and slanted eyes (especially when she smiled, lol). Surprisingly, P was loud and outgoing—not typical for Asian culture. We clicked because of the whole Blasian girl who likes to party thing.

Once more people started to arrive, the men noticed I was new. You remember when you were a freshman, and the older guys could sniff you out for some reason? Yeah, it was a lot like that. BUT admittingly, I liked it. What?! Just keeping it real. Well-groomed men surrounding you with good laughs would give any woman a confidence boost. So, don't judge me!

From that point on, we'd meet practically every weekend and for happy hours during the weekday. It was like we worked hard...well, worked *kinda* hard... and partied hard. Yeah, we definitely partied hard!

~Alert~ *One hour until the surprise party for Dave.*

It was so cute how the girlfriend (can't remember her name, so we will just call her GF for short) put that all together. She created a secret group chat and was plotting away. I couldn't help but wonder (in my Carrie Bradshaw voice) when I'll have someone in my life that I could do that for. Hmmm... (deep sigh)

Let me get off the couch and get ready before I'm late.

Now for the dilemma: attire. Y'all know I'm not the only one who's like, *what am I going to wear*? It's like you want to be cute, but not club cute. Then, it's at an adult arcade. So, you want to be cute enough to play games and shoot pool, but not have your hoo-ha busted wide open, catching a breeze.

Let me take another sip of my honey whiskey and apple juice—that should help me get my mind right. Yes, I said honey whiskey with apple juice. Try it! You will literally not taste the alcohol WHATSOEVER. It's muey delicioso!

Ahhh... refreshing.

Okay. *I, am, gonna, wear...these jeans that make my butt look cute and round while showing my thigh definition. Uh-huh. Yep! That red top and some sandals since God blessed me with pretty feet.* As Cardi B would say, *"Eeeeoooooww!"*

So, I finally got to the arcade and headed straight to the bar. You know, like any sane person would do. I saw one of the guys, Morris, from the Meetup already there.

Now, Morris was a chocolate, 6'3-ish, nice full-lipped, big-handed man with a fade, kind of snack. When he said, "Hey, what's up?" I was all like, "Heyyy," in my cute flirty voice. "What are you drinking?"

Right when I was about to *really* get my flirt on, another guy came up and interrupted our session. After giving dabs to Morris, he turned to me and was like, "Hi, I'm Judas."

Me: "Oh, *you're* Judas. Hi, I'm Jenn."

Judas: "Oh, *you're* Jenn B. Nice to finally meet you."

Me: "Lol. Yeah...you too."

Back story: we were in the group chat, and he literally made me laugh out loud with his comments. So, I indulged Judas with some chit chat. I noticed Morris left the bar; however, I will admit Judas was cute. Welp, I'm just going with the flow.

We walked to the table area where the official surprise was taking place. I saw my girls Chris and Jane and popped a squat next to them.

Okay, so Jane was that typical thick white girl who liked black guys and basically lived with her parents. She had long brown hair, fluffy in the backside, loved to drink, and was a good time because she was always down. ALWAYS. She was also secretly sleeping with Jamar as a side bitch for several months while his girlfriend lived out of town. It ended after she caught some real feelings—or should I say Jamar ended it. But hey, that's none of my business.

Now Chris is also a white girl with dirty blonde hair. She's a hipster chick who smokes weed, only dates men of color, and has lost like a hundred pounds. I am so proud and impressed with her dedication. She was looking good! After we greeted each other, guess who sat directly across from me? Like, I blinked, and there that nigga was: Judas! It took me by surprise, but I figured that may be his first Meetup event. I indulged him in conversation, and then he went to get a refill at the bar. The next thing I knew, Chris and Jane were ready for the tea.

Chris: "Judas is cute, huh?"

Me (looking like this): "Yyyeah..." (it was one of those what's your point, why you asking, and what are y'all up to kinda yeah's)

Jane (her two cents): "Y'all just seem to be hitting it off is all."

Me: "Yeah, I suppose... he's cute and funny."

I didn't get where they were going with that, but it almost seemed like it was a setup. Either that, or they were trying to hook us up or something. Apparently, they already knew him, so that wasn't his first Meetup.

But I just left it.

After a while, Dave arrived blindfolded. That nigga is over 6 foot, fair-skinned, and fluffy. Just picture him being blindfolded as he walked into D&B and turned super red when we all yelled, "*Surprise!!!!*" Ha!

Nonetheless, we were all happy to be a part of the surprise and celebrate his birthday. He was a cool and likable dude.

As you may know, after you turn 21, most gifts consist of friends buying you drinks. Sooooooo, that's exactly what happened. I witnessed at least 10 transactions, and I was only there for a few hours! Most of my time there, I was caught chatting with or near Judas. It was clear he was trying to get to know me, and I entertained it—so, I can't blame him 100%. Only 90%. Ha!

CHAPTER 1

The next day, and I mean *the very* next day, I got a direct solo message from none other than that Judas. I will admit it was cute and manlike to pursue and be consistent. So, I responded with a "Hi" back. Don't worry; it wasn't immediately. I waited a bit before I responded. Yes, I played the game.

He proceeded to invite me to the movies. I accepted but chose the theater by my house, so I didn't have to drive far. He was cool with that– not that he really had a choice.

The next week we had our first date. Surprisingly, we meshed extremely well, and he kept me laughing.

He was a gentleman. He opened doors, made sure he was walking closer to the street as if he was being protective, and was even sincere when he asked me if I wanted some popcorn. You know sometimes people just ask as a courtesy. Even though I declined, he still bought me a small bag anyways. So, I ate some. Lol.

He walked me back to the car, and we stood there chatting it up. His body language showed he was engaged and even more interested. Eventually, I started to feel a little chilly, so we thought it best to call it a night, but not before he moved in for the kiss. It's so sexy when a man just *knows* the right time. When he can feel the CORRECT vibes and doesn't bother to ask. He just does it. He did it quite well, too, if I might add. Had me feeling some kind of way.... It was nice. Really nice.

Needless to say, he was constantly texting me multiple times throughout the day. He was really, *really* interested. But let's not get it twisted, he was NOT the only one on the roster.

There was that guy Ken that I wasn't really sexually attracted to. Morris came into play at one point. Then there was Anthony, who I've known for like seven years and never got physical with. Chris was serving our country in the Navy. Last but not least, we had Zachary with the bomb head.

Ken is a black guy from D.C. and worked in real estate. Real estate was something I was considering, so it was good to connect with him. He was sweet, kept me laughing, and worked near my house. We often went to happy hours mid-week together. And yes, every time we went, the tab was always on him—just like a gentleman ought to do. Downside: he was only like 5'3. IDK... to me, it's weird looking at a man at eye level.

On top of that, he wore braces! Even though he was getting them taken off in like a month, it was sooo distracting. Like my mind kept wondering if he went down on me, would he scratch my vagina. That is a legit question! It was just too much. Undeniably, Ken was just one of those you kept around for good laughs during the week. Plus, if I needed a real estate job, I networked with him on a professional level too. Smart, huh?

Morris from the Meetup eventually came into play. Remember, he was the one at the bar who was like 6'1 and chocolate with a fade. He worked in IT, so that benefitted me when I needed some local technical assistance, you know? He really was an African sweetheart. At least to me, anyway. I did hear he dogged some girl out in VIP, though. Yikes!

Next, there was Anthony. I met Anthony circa 2008 at the Taste of Chicago. I was on a girl's trip, and he was visiting his family with his boys. Anthony played football in college and then overseas. After a year or two, he returned to the states to coach college ball. He was also a member of the Omega Psi Phi fraternity incorporated, AKA the Ques. Ladies, I'm sure y'all already know what's up when it comes to those Ques.

Then, a few years back, when I moved to Virginia Beach after college graduation, I met Chris through mutual friends who were in the military like him. One of the girls I knew, who was cheating on her husband, invited Chris over for a get-together. I noticed him but didn't know how much I'd see him since I was so busy doing other things. So, I didn't go beyond flirting. After that, I started to see him on a regular. My interest was piqued, so I asked my friend Tisha what his deal was. Apparently, he was recently divorced with a son. She knew this because they worked together in the Navy in the IT department. In other words, she knew his whole life. Eventually, I allowed him to be a part of the roster. Not too long after, he became MVP for like an entire year and a half. Chris was such a good dad. Even though his ex had full custody, like clockwork, he'd visit his son and help with homework every single day after work. Once he was done, he still wouldn't leave until he tucked little man in the bed. That alone turned me on—being a military man who was fathering. Yes, fathering, like a verb. In other words, he was doing what fathers *should* do. Hm, yass!

Y'all know what else turned me on? His bald head and those juicy lips. He was such an amazing kisser. No, scratch that. He was an incredible kisser. Probably the best I've ever had. We could've made out for days, but it didn't take long before I needed more. Y'all know what I mean. Those kisses that got you moist. Then somehow, someone ended up on top of the other caressing and nibbling the ear, necking, and finger popping. Then, again, somehow, clothes would start to fall off. Oh, em gee... I still remember our first time. His curved dick took me by surprise. A *good* surprise at that. Our first time was like 4 hours. 4 hours just full of kisses, grabs, biting, deep strokes, sucking, and licking. It was a real workout now that I think about it. And if y'all have ever had a curved dick....whoa!! Shitttt, I'm about to get wet just thinking about him and that dick. Shit!

Deep sigh. Let's move on...

So, by this day and age, people were meeting online and through apps. I know y'all are familiar with dating websites and apps. The whole swipe left if he ain't cute and swipe right if you can get with that routine. That brings me to Zachary.

Our first date was at that new low-key hookah bar that was around the corner from my house that I didn't know about. Come to find out, he lived like three lights away from me. Uh-oh is right. So over time (I'm not going to say how much time), I discovered that nigga loves to eat. I am not talking about eating his grand momma's mac & cheese. I am talking about he loved to put his face in between my legs and lick, suck, slurp and finger that pussy!

Mmm! Mm! Mm! As a matter of fact, let me text him *raight* now and see if he's free tonight. He's what you would call, my beck and call nigga. AND the fact he lived so close made it even sweeter.

Even though I'm already sweet, warm, juicy, and succulent like pie. IJS!

CHAPTER 2

So, I guess it's time to answer the burning question. What did Judas look like? Well, he's black. His mom was from Trinidad and his dad from Panama—not the city in Florida but the country. That explained his looks. Judas was around 5'10, chocolate skinned tone, fit and defined with skinny legs, curly mohawk, thick lips, and big hands. Y'all know the hands are important.

Judas was really funny. He was an HR professional at a well-known international home furnishing store (I can't disclose who since I'm not getting endorsed from them. IJS). He had a daughter from a previous relationship several years ago, which didn't bother me. He was a gentleman, strong, respectful, helped his mother do yard work regularly, sent her on vacations since she was practically a single mom, a Christian, personable, easy to like and be around, and finally the only child like me.

After a while, I invited Judas over for dinner. Since it was a workday, I didn't do anything too fancy. I decided on a chicken Caesar wrap and homemade fries. Oh yeah, and of course, wine. He was the typical guy who didn't cook, so I was sure he'd appreciate the meal. I didn't want to go all out since, you know, we weren't in a committed monogamous relationship. So, I went ahead and washed, seasoned, and baked the chicken breast. (I mentioned the washed part because apparently, not everyone is aware they should wash the chicken before eating it... Y'all know who I'm talking about). Next, I cut the potatoes, seasoned them real good, and then placed them in the oven. I figured it would cook while I took a quick shower (you never know what could happen). Once I hopped out of the shower, I got a text saying, "be there in 5 min".

OMG! I was frantic, to say the least. I quickly put my smell goods on, a pair of leggings, and a t-shirt. Yes, y'all.

Loungewear. I didn't want to look like I tried TOO hard. We are at my house on a workday, so don't forget that.

The next thing I knew... *ding dong, ding dong!* 😐 Omg, *he was here!*

I opened the door.

Judas: "Hey!"

Me: "Hi- come in!"

<hugs>

Judas: "Is something burning?"

<I took a quick sniff sniff>

Me: "Oh, no! Oh, no!"

I rushed over to the kitchen and pulled out the fries.

Me: "Oh, nooooooo!!!! I cannot believe I forgot the potatoes in the oven. And they burned! Aww, man..."

At that point, I was feeling embarrassed because I RARELY burn food.

Judas: "Well, maybe they aren't that burnt," he said as he walked towards the oven and paused. "Uh, yep, those are burnt," he laughed.

Me: "Omg, I am so sorry! That never happens..."

I could feel my cheeks turning red of embarrassment.

Judas: "It's ok. At least you can still make the wraps. And I brought the drinks."

A drink is what I needed to calm down too.

Me: "Okay, let me turn the vent on."

I poured us drinks, and he sat waiting on the wraps.

I quickly thought of a plan B.

Me: "Do you want chips and salsa?" I asked.

Judas: "Sure."

Yes, chips and salsa to the rescue!

Both of us: "We can eat it with the wraps instead of the fries."

I was glad we were on the same page.

I made his plate, and we sat on the couch so we could watch TV while we ate.

Judas: "Sooo that is how you look at night?"

Me: "What do you mean?" I asked, thinking he was talking about my leggings and white tee.

Judas: "With your hair wrapped up in your scarf."

Me: "Huh?"

I felt the top of my head and was mortified. I put my face down with even more embarrassment. *Could things get any worse?* I thought. I seriously needed to get it together. *Ok, Jenn, don't let him see you sweat.*

Me: "Yep, I forgot I still had it on. But if we continue, then you'd see me with my hair wrapped eventually, no?"

Yes, play it cool.

Judas: "True, but it's cool. You're still pretty."

"Thanks," I said blushing.

With that, we ate, drank, talked, and watched some TV. Then, he decided he wanted to spend the night. Yes, he just invited himself...but I guess I was okay with it.

He got undressed down to his briefs.

Judas: "I get hot easily."

Me: "Mm-hm," I smirked.

He started to wrap his hands around me like he was trying to cuddle.

[Sidenote: I am not a snuggler. It's like... where do you put your arm? Is my head too heavy? Why am I sweating? My arm is falling asleep. At the same time, you don't want to move; otherwise, the other person may think you don't want to be bothered. Ugh, y'all feel me, right?? Plus, I feel like that's really intimate. Intimacy was something I didn't embrace very often.]

However, even with ALL those thoughts, for some reason or another, it felt okay. Like it was meant to be or something.

Judas: "I'm a social sleeper."

Me (chuckling): "I have literally never heard of that before. Good one."

Somehow, we started to make out. (I know what you're thinking, but yes somehow is right.) He was such a good kisser that I couldn't resist.

Eventually, I started to rub. He started to rub. The rubbing turned into caressing. The caressing turned into caressing with intent. And of course, that started the juices to flow.

Y'all know he was trynna get inside to finger pop. But nope! I did NOT give in. I kept pushing his hands away.

Then... after a few hours... I kept thinking about how big and strong his hands were. How good of a kisser he was. And y'all know I slid my hands from his chest down to his stomach and further down—just to get a quick feel of his dick. Mm! I was trynna be slick.

So, I did what any woman would do. I backed that ass up. I scooted my booty over to his dick. I did a little swirl, swirl. 😁 You know, as if I was just repositioning myself to get comfy. In all actuality, I was clearly seeing if he was awake. *Oh kurrrr!* (credit to Cardi B).

Once I felt him 1) grip me and 2) get hard (all within like 2 seconds btw), we started to make out again. Y'all don't understand how awesome of a kisser he was. Did I mention that already?

Anyways, then he got on top and began to kiss down to my toes and brought it back up. BUT, not before he made a pitstop. 😌

He gently kissed my inner thigh while caressing and clutching my ass. Then while kissing my inner thigh, he got closer and closer to my pussy. Moments later, he tasted my pussy for the first time. He licked my clit softly up and down, swirling his tongue in circles, and inserted his tongue inside my now even wetter pussy. He slid his tongue in and out. In and out. In and out. He grabbed my hips and ass to pull me even closer so I could fuck his tongue. Unconsciously, I began to maneuver my hips back and forth. Forcing his tongue to go deeper and deeper until his nose was moistened by my clit. Mmmmmm.....

His tongue tricks were magical.

Breathing hard and still kissing....

At that point, I had no choice. I took off his briefs and pulled out his massive hard dick.

All I kept hearing was that Jill Scott's "Crown Royal" song: *"Your hands on my hips pull me right back to you, I catch that thrust give it right back to you. You're in so deep I'm breathing for you. ..I flip shit, quick slip, hip dip and I'm twisted... your tongue tricks and you're so thick.. crown royal on ice.*" If you don't know this song, you should go listen to it....like right now though. It is amazing!

He was incredible at performing cunnilingus (trying to sound politically correct, but that shit sounds weird AF). But yeah, he was sooooo incredible at it.

I couldn't tell before how big he was because y'all know how deceiving briefs can be. Everyone looked big in them—from the tree stubs to the half pencil dicks. When I did that quick feel, he clearly wasn't 100% hard and had an unexpected one.

Okay, can I also just say it is EXTREMELY rare to find someone who has a big dick AND gives awesome head. RARE I TELL YA! RARE!

Me: "Omg, what time is it? Do I have time–"

Judas: "For round 2," he said, cutting me off.

I giggled and checked my phone. "Ugh, I've got to leave in an hour."

Judas: "That's enough time."

He pulled me to the edge of the bed, spread 'em wide open, and stuffed his face in between my legs. In all the right places too.

Then, I couldn't help it AGAIN, so I pulled his face up and demanded that dick.

As I bit his bottom lip, he inserted the tip of his dick slowly. He teased me with just the tip until I finally moved my hips closer to him and swirled my hips around his dick as if his dick was a pole I was spinning on. And well frankly, it was a pole I was gyrating around.

Needless to say, I was late to work that day.

CHAPTER 3

So, I am gonna keep it 100. From our dinner date on, we spent more and more time together, leaving little room for others. You already know that I still had those others in my pocket though.

We did agree to keep—whatever it was—just between us since it was still new, and we had too many mutual friends. We didn't want everyone in our business. Not just yet, anyway.

We continued to go on dates and hang out with the Meetup Group multiple times weekly. Once Judas finally got a new place, he invited me over. He was all like, "Yeah, I finally got my spot, and I want you to be the first to come over. Not even my mom has visited yet. Plus, I want to cook *you* dinner this time."

I was so excited, and yes, it made me feel special too. Of course, I accepted his invitation.

Friday after work, I GPS-ed to Judas's new spot. It was only like 3.5 miles away in Buckhead, but with that Atlanta traffic, that took away like 30 minutes of my life.

I pulled up into the parking garage, and he buzzed me in. Already at that point, I could tell his apartment was nicer than mine. You see, I had no parking garage, and I did not live in no Buckhead.

Well anyway, he came out to the garage and greeted me with a booty grab and a kiss. And I liked it or whatever.

He opened his apartment door, and I was impressed. There were granite countertops, high-quality carpet, a big bathroom, a workstation, and a huge walk-in closet. It was definitely Buckhead worthy. And it was clean and organized. Bonus points.

Judas: "I only have 2 rules."

Me: "Ook..."

Judas: "1) No shoes in the house. But that's normal for you since you're Asian."

Me: "Ha!"

Judas: "2) You can eat/drink whatever, just let me know it's the last of it so I don't go looking for it and it ain't even there."

Me: "Ok, cool, I can respect that... can you pour me a drink now?"

He finally poured the wine.

"So, what are you gonna cook? I was shocked you wanted to cook because I thought you didn't know how to cook anything."

Judas: "Yeah, I don't."

Me (looking like 💀): "Ummmm, ok...."

Judas (chuckling): "Except this one thing. My favorite meal."

Me: "Uh, ok. Now I'm scared."

Judas: "Don't be. It's good, and I like it."

Me: "Just tell me what it is already!"

Judas: "Chicken tenders, rice, and mix vegetables."

Me: "Now, I'm even more confused." 💀

Judas laughed and pulled out frozen chicken tender strips, frozen mixed veggies, and a bag of rice.

I was literally LMAO!!!!!!! This was pure comedy!

After I caught my breath from laughing so damn hard, I offered to help. He was all like, "Nah, I got this. You just sit back and relax."

Me: "Ok, you got it then."

He then proceeded to put the bag of unopened, uncooked rice in a pot of boiling water... so I interrupted him.

Me: "What are you doing?!"

Judas: "Making rice."

Me: "But it's still in the plastic. You're just going to put it in the water like that?!?"

Judas: "Yeah, you're supposed to."

Me: "Uh, no you're not."

Judas: "Yeah, look at the directions on the box."

Me: "That is so weird! I have literally never heard nor seen anything like this. That makes no sense! How does the rice cook without water?! I am so confused... I don't get it whatsoever."

Meanwhile, he was cracking up because I was legitimately perplexed.

Judas: "Trust me, it cooks perfectly every time. You're only confused because you're Asian and only know how to cook rice in a rice cooker."

Me: "Haha, very funny nigga."

We continued to talk, and he continued to "cook." Once it was finished, he made our plates.

Me: "Are you going to season the food?"

He proceeded to make the plates and handed me the salt.

Judas: "I usually just put salt on the food while it's on the plate."

Me: "Oooh kay."

So, I sprinkled salt and pepper over the veggies and rice.

Now the rice looked... well, wet and soggy, which btw I didn't know how that was even possible because the plastic bag was sealed. IDK. It still didn't make sense, but whatever.

He must have noticed my facial expression as I was picking at the rice and observing it.

Judas: "I think I cooked the rice too long."

Me: "Mm yeah maybe, IDK how it's supposed to taste," I giggled, "but everything else is ok."

I didn't want it to look like I didn't appreciate his efforts because it was still a sweet gesture.

"And the wine is DE-LI-CIOUS. Well done! Cheers!"

I didn't eat much. Not because it was disgusting, but because I was full off the wine.

Eh, it happens.

We snuggled on the couch, and before you know it, we were making out.

Somehow, I ended up sitting on his lap while he was embracing... well, all of me. The kisses grew more passionate. Then, those kisses started to migrate downward. A bit of ear nibbling. A little necking. More fondling for sure.

By that point, his dick was bulging out of his pants. Soooo, I figured I'd give it some more space.

Now from what you know of me thus far, I know you may find it hard to believe; but one way or another, I started to unbutton his pants and noticed his dick in my mouth. IKR! Difficult to fathom. (What I meant by "giving it more space". LOL)

Nevertheless, his dick *did* find its way inside my mouth. So, I did what any woman would do. I sucked it! I swirled my tongue around the tip, slid that thang towards my throat, stroked, tea bagged his balls, and well... frankly... handled it.

He eventually took me into his bedroom to bang the fuck out of my pussy. Keep in mind, the last time we slept together was at my house before I had to rush off to work. There were some built-up emotions to be dealt with if you know what I mean.

And we ....*erupted* through those feelings for the next couple of hours too. Hehe...

Before we could doze off, I started to get dressed.

Judas: "Where are you going?"

Me: "Home."

Judas: "Why?"

Me: "What do you mean why?

Judas: "Why don't you just stay the night."

Me: "I didn't bring anything."

Judas: "Well, you can go get stuff if you want and come back or leave in the morning and come back?"

Me: "Aww, you don't want me to leave, huh? That's cute."

Judas: "No, I really don't.."

Me: "Ok, I'll get an overnight bag and come back."

Judas: "Cool."

He walked me to the car, we kissed, and I drove off to return.

A shower and an hour later, I had on the classic leggings and white tee combo.

In my bag was my silk scarf, sundress, extra panties, and toiletries, of course. Then I headed back, feeling all happy and shit.

A lot of niggas (and females) tend to say, "Don't leave, I want you to stay," but don't mean it. This was different, though. Judas was being sincere. He really enjoyed my company, you know. And I enjoyed his too, to be honest.

.

.

.

So, I returned to his house, and he greeted me in the garage again. We walked inside as he carried my overnight bag. *Such a gentleman,* I thought to myself. With all the events that happened today, I just couldn't help myself. I just started making out with him *AGAIN!* Then one thing led to another, clothes came off, our breaths got quicker, pussy got wetter, dick got harder, and well... y'all know what happened next.

Afterward, I hopped in the shower. It was spotless clean, too—just the way I liked it. I took a step in and heard the door slowly open. I peeked from the shower curtain, and it was Judas!

(It didn't occur to me I needed to lock the door.)

Me: "Heyyy, what are you doing!?"

Judas: "Joining you."

Me: "Ummmm.."

Now THAT right there was really ummmmm.... IDK how I felt. Because although we just had sex, I always thought showering together was really intimate. I've only showered with one man, maybe like 3x total. Y'all remember Chris with the curved dick and the superb tongue game? Yeah, it was with him.

Well, anyway, I didn't know how I felt ...

Even so, I allowed it to happen anyway. *Is he being bold and manly? Or is he beginning to fall for me like the rest of them? Or is it some weird combination of both? OR maybe I was just overthinking it. Ok, snap out of it!*

Anyway, I'm sure this goes without saying, but that intimate shower moment led to conversations, and then a little bit of dick sucking. Just a smudge. What?!? His dick was nice and fresh. IJS! The steam got to me or something.

When we finally got out of the shower, I proceeded to put on some lotion, and he grabbed the bottle from me and rubbed the lotion on my feet. He even massaged lotion into my legs and my back y'all! IDK what he was up to, but that was a first for me. Ain't no man ever put lotion on my whole body after a shower and not expect sex immediately afterwards. Like it was a form of foreplay or something.

Judas was super sweet and caring. He was certainly making me feel special and trying to win me over.

We eventually got into bed and fell right to sleep. A few hours later, I woke up to urinate and swooshed around some mouth wash. I was in a dick-sucking mood. Sooooo I went back in the bed to snuggle up with him. Then, I "accidentally" swiped my hand across his dick, slid my hand down his chest and stomach, just to take off his drawers. He let me, of course. Once I pulled out his dick, he was already somewhat hard. At that point, I did the only thing left to do: I slid his dick in my wet refreshed mouth and opened as wide as I could, so I could put as much of it in my mouth as possible.

By the time I pulled it out, it was massively hard. Pointing straight up to the ceiling and ready for me.

Do y'all remember those long rainbow twisty lollipops? Well, I sucked on that thang like it was a unicorn lollipop. I spun my tongue around. I licked it. I basically turned my mouth into a live suction... hole (not cup).

After a while, I did my finale. I flipped back over to my side of the bed, did a little booty wiggle to get comfy, and he came up to my ear saying, "Oh, you're not getting away that easy."

I'm sure you can guess what happened after that.

We eventually fell right back to sleep. In the morning, he woke me up with a good morning kiss.

Now IDK about y'all, but I need eggs in the morning.

So, we got up, and I went for the kitchen. I found some eggs and asked if he wanted any. He showed me the turkey bacon, and I went to work.

To my surprise, that nigga wanted like 7 pieces of bacon. Correction: turkey bacon.

When I was making breakfast, I told him he needed to go grocery shopping because his pantry AND fridge were extremely empty. He was all like, "I know, we should go grocery shopping." "*We*?!" I said aloud. He laughed, "Yes, *we.*"

All I could do was say, "OK."

We got ready, and he drove us to that well-known farmer's market on the east side of Atlanta (that I can't mention by name since they aren't endorsing me. IJS, again.).

Anyways, I had always heard about how great it was but had never been. Probably because I don't live in the perimeter or ITP, as some say.

Meanwhile, I stepped out of the car and felt something wet on my booty. So, I checked the seat and myself. Guess what you guys?!? That nigga made my period start early!

Oh! Em! Gee! I had on a blue maxi skirt with a split and a crop top. I thought I was cute up until that madness!

Ok, think, I thought to myself. *And quickly before he comes around the corner!*

Luckily a lightbulb went off. *Turn the skirt around and hold the bottom up to the middle as if it were too long. I hope he doesn't notice. Yikes, here he comes!*

He came over and said, "Come on, you look great." *Whew, that was a relief. Thank you, Jesus!*

Y'all know I kept checking myself. Ugh, that was sooooo embarrassing!

In the interim, I helped him pick out the fruit and veggies. He wanted to be cute and show me the entire store. So, he took me to the little Korean section. "Haha, very funny nigga," I proclaimed.

Then we walked way past the checkout lines. I was like, "There's checkout." Y'all know I was trying to get him to speed things up because I still had that situation going on and had to keep it hidden. *Deep sigh!*

He took me to the seafood area with the live fresh fish swimming in the tanks. IDK why, but that made me elated.

How did he know?!? #lame #corny #idc #allsmiles 😌

We FINALLY got back to the house, and I ran to the restroom and pretended like I JUST started my period at that very moment.

Luckily, I had a backup outfit and tampons in my overnight bag. But changed into leggings because it- was-naptime!

We snuggled on his couch. It was oh so comfy, and I fit right in securely.

[Sidenote: Do you guys think cuddling can be cumbersome like I do? It's like, "Where do you put your head? Is my head too heavy? Where do I put my arm? Oh no, now my arm is falling asleep. Omg, I'm about to start sweating..." Seeeeee it's toooo much, which is why I just avoid it altogether. Oh right, I've already mentioned that. Well, it is that important.]

But for some reason or another, I:

1. Gave in to the cuddle sessions with him.
2. Liked it.
3. And stayed cuddled for a long period of time. Comfortably.

That was a HUGE deal! Somebody knows what I'm talking about.... Right?!?

Anyways...

The TV was on, but I fell right to sleep. Yes, both he and it were that cozy.

As I was sleep, I could feel him kiss my forehead too. I thought to myself, *Aww, that's sweet*. Actually, Girls Special's blog about forehead kisses mentioned that forehead kisses "are endearing, more emotional, a sign of sincere feelings that he cares about you, more intimate; essentially occurs when there's a deep bond or connection." It's true. Look it up.

After a while, we both woke up.

He decided he wanted to make his favorite snack for me: cheese and crackers. Lol! So what pairs best with cheese and crackers? If you said, "Wine," then you're my people!

Luckily, I had brought the sangria since he had originally invited me over for dinner the night before.

Eventually, those cheese and crackers were not cutting it, so we ordered from his favorite pizza place. They were those huge NY style slices, and he ate like 3 slices! That nigga could *eat*. And since I'm like a big-picture thinker, I was like all our money would go towards groceries. Geesh.

Ultimately night rolled around, so we hit the streets. But not before a quick pre-game of my favorite: tequila!

He took me to that local place up the street that had $2 fireball shots. Naturally, we took some of those and then hit the dance floor. We loved to dance. The more drinks we accumulated, the more the music became appealing.

Shortly after the $2 shots ended, we moved on to Crescent Ave., a popular bar-hopping street in the heart of the city.

I loved the fact we didn't have to go to a hood spot that only played ratchet and trap music to have fun. We could have fun and dance to pop music like Ed Sheeran, Taylor Swift, Maroon 5...etc.

Since I was still new to Atlanta, he wanted to show me some spots. For instance, we stopped at a dessert café nearby. He didn't know at the time, but I didn't really like desserts. I mean, I don't like chocolate, nuts, peanut butter, icing, cream filling, sprinkles, or syrup. So what's the point? He was so excited to take me there, though. I felt bad that I didn't order anything, but we sat outside while he ate. I fed him a bite or 2 to make it a bit special.

We continued on our mini adventure towards drunkenness and continued to dance the night away.

Now for these types of bars/clubs, the crowd started dwindling down early. So, we migrated further south to that hood spot that was popular on Camp Creek. It took a little minute to get there, but during the ride, he proceeded to open up about his feelings towards me.

Judas: "So I probably shouldn't tell you this, but...."

Me: "Now, you have to tell me!"

Judas: "... I am ... falling... in like with you..."

Me: "In like?!"

Judas: "Yeah. Like I really like you, but not to the point I'm in love with you yet. But we mesh well, have good vibes, have the same values, and are headed in the same direction, I feel. Plus, I know I fall in love quickly."

Me: "Hmmmm... yeah, I could see that.... Us meshing well together- that's true..."

Was he just drunk talking, or was he for real? I guess time will tell.... I said to myself.

Whew! Luckily, we arrived before there was a chance to possibly have any awkward silence.

He came around and opened my door (as a real man should), and we walked inside. He went to the bathroom while I headed straight to the bar.

I noticed a few people had blue pitchers and asked someone how much those were.

Y'all are not gonna believe it. They were only $10!!!!! Yes, only a whopping $10! In Atlanta, that is stupid cheap for a drink—especially one in a pitcher.

Needless to say, we ordered 2 and continued to dance the night away ... with a few make out sessions in the corner... again.

Eventually, they shut the place down, and we were forced to head back to his house.

Sadly / Enjoyably, I fell asleep on the ride back. What?!? Even though I felt bad for falling asleep on him because he had no one to talk to during the drive, it felt soooo good. Plus, I literally had no choice or control over myself. My body sat down and was knocked out almost instantly. I blame it on the alcohol, as Jaime Foxx would say. Sometimes it just be like that, though.

ANYWAYS, when we arrived back to his house, the weather felt so nice out. As a result, we took a stroll to the courtyards. There were benches, swings, flowers, and a waterfall. It was so cute. He lived in a high rise, shaped like a rectangle. In essence, the apartment was the perimeter, and within it was the pool and the courtyard.

Similar to this:

We popped a squat on the bench swing thingy, and he proceeded to pick up his discussion about his feelings for me.

Judas: "I may be speaking too soon, but I can see something from this."

Me: "Oh, really?"

Judas: "Yeah, so far... but I want to make more money for my family. I mean, even with the child support for my daughter, Janelle. I do alright, but I've been with this company for 9 years, and my boss is not retiring anytime soon. And her position is the next step in my career."

[Sidenote: He started with that company building the kitchens and then somehow worked his way up to an HR Generalist role in a few short years. So, he has been in the HR field for a while. Sometimes he would manage the Director duties when she didn't want to show up for work—which seemed like almost every other week. It was impressive for sure.]

Me: "So what's the plan because I do want a dog and the white picket fence and all that..."

Judas (laughing): "Yeah, I want to be able to provide that for you and our family. And more."

Me: "That's a good goal. .... So you have a daughter?"

Judas: "Yes, she's 8 now."

He took out his phone to show me a pic.

Me: "Aw, she's pretty. Where is she?"

Judas: "With her mom."

Me: "Oh, I see."

Judas: "Yeah, that's my baby. I wish I could see her every day, but she lives in North Carolina."

Me: "Oh..."

I could tell he was feeling a way, so I didn't push the subject, but he continued anyway.

Judas: "Yeah, we were in a relationship and had her when I was 21 still in school. That's why it's been taking me so long to finish and graduate because I had to provide. But she's my heart."

I could tell he was sad and missing his baby girl. It was also really sweet how he'd light up like a proud papa when he spoke of her. It was endearing. Obviously, he loved her with his whole being—just as he should. It was super sad that they didn't live in the same city to spend more time together though. A girl needs a father. These days there was Facetime to fill some of the void, but I didn't know if it was enough. I hoped he visited her often.

There was a non-awkward silence while a summer night's breeze flew by.

Judas: "But yeah, I want to be able to provide."

Me: "Provide like... I don't have to work, but we still have the nice house, fence, dog, and a pair of Christian Louboutin's?"

Judas: "All of that. But I'd want to give you more than just 1 pair of red bottoms. Just in case the dog eats a shoe."

He put my legs on his lap and swung us. It just felt so good outside I didn't want to go in, but the yawns were nonstop. I mean by that point, it was like 4:00 a.m.

So, we headed off to bed.

.

.

.

Nooooo, no sex. I started my period. Remember that whole debacle earlier?

.

.

.

Maybe a few hours later, I heard Judas calling his boss. Essentially, he was telling her that he wasn't coming that day. He had said he rarely took his PTO and had over 100 hours, which was impressive.

I could tell by his responses that she was asking if everything was okay. In other words, she was trying to get to the root of why he was calling off. But Judas did not specify. He told her if things changed later that afternoon that he'd call to let her know he was coming in, but it depended on his headache.

[Sidenote: If you're calling off, you do not have to provide a reason. If you have the time to take, it's yours to take. It's not mandatory for you to tell your employer the reason(s). I mean, unless it's specified in the policy that you signed as a new hire or if you feel compelled.]

He stayed at the house with me watching movies and sports, napping on the couch, cuddling, ...etc.

While we were snacking, it came across my mind that we had spent the entire weekend together. And it went well. Like *really* well. For me, that was a HUGE deal because I can get annoyed being cooped up with someone for an entire weekend.

As I had my mouth open to express these thoughts, he uttered literally just what I was thinking.

Judas: "Have you noticed we spent the entire weekend together?"

Me: "Omg, yes! I was literally just thinking the same exact thing! And..."

Both of us (simultaneously): "...that's weird because usually I get annoyed."

We both laughed.

Me: "That's crazy!"

Judas: "Yeah, it is... but I like it."

He kissed me and made me another drink.

Eventually, I packed up and went back home. Grinning from ear to ear as I thought how special this guy was.

CHAPTER 4

Remember, Judas and I met through the Meetup Group, and they met up on a weekly basis.

Well, once Judas got settled in officially, his clubhouse became the pre-game spot. But not without my help. He invited them, and WE setup to host.

He reserved the space, bought all the disposables, and then I'd show up early for our own pre-game. Everyone else would bring a bottle. After a couple of hours, it would be time to hit the streets. His place was the perfect spot to share a ride anywhere.

Everyone had good vibes... always. No one had drama or arguments. No one was an angry, boo-hoo crying drunk either. We were all happy drunks who liked to party, dance, laugh, and make good memories.

Like a third of the time, Judas and I'd sneak off to "put the cups away." In reality, we'd really be making out, eating, finger-popping, talking about other people.... You know, getting a little us time in.

It didn't occur to me in the beginning, but almost every other weekend, we hosted pre-game sessions at his clubhouse.

I hoped no one noticed we were always together. We both agreed we wanted to keep whatever it was to ourselves for now.

I'll never forget that one time when we snuck up to his apartment and just moments later, John, his friend, and the girlfriend, Heather, came knocking at the door. Judas quickly pulled his pants up, and I pulled my skirt up.

So, he opened the door, and I hid in the bathroom. Judas told me to come out because they already knew about us.

I was like, "What?! I thought this was a secret." He just shrugged his shoulders and walked away.

Smh.

Well, I could tell Heather had too much to drink because she was trying to get freaky with John.

I quickly shut that down and told everyone we should go. So, we headed out to meet the others.

Per usual, we always rolled deep, so you could find half at the bar and the other half on the dance floor. Eventually, everyone ended up on the dance floor though.

Ultimately, people and couples would start to disperse. Others like myself and Judas would go find food at Waffle House or Cookout. I'll never forget Judas taking a photo of me killing a burger and then posting in the group chat for all to see. It was *slightly* embarrassing, but it is what it is.

_jenuine

Aaaah, good times!

When we finally made it back to his house, we'd do one of the following:

1. Pass out
2. Have sex, *then* pass out
3. Pass out, have sex, then pass out again

Aaaah, even better times!

Now on the days there were no public pregame sessions, Judas and I would have our own pregame. Since I loved tequila (and still do), we'd do tequila shots with the salt and lime. Y'all know how it goes-- salt, shot, lime baby!

So we'd do a few of those. Yes...just a few.

When we were in the car, somehow or another, my head would end up in his lap. My mouth would be wide open--

slurping, licking, and sucking his dick. A dick that just so happen to be out like it was a popsicle on a hot summer day in Miami. I just... IDK.

We used to meet people at art shows, clubs, and happy hours all over the city.

Basically, we were in the streets on a weekly basis. We used to arrive AND leave together.

There was one time, Judas's best friend and co-worker, Nick (I say his friend, but he was my friend too), had to stay over because he was too drunk. I know I said it was supposed to be a secret, but it's okay. He knew all about Judas and I. Judas went to work, and Nick stayed behind. I made breakfast and put him on to a TV series about a wealthy distributor who was trying to get out the game but ended up cheating on his wife with his childhood sweetheart. It was such a good show. From that point on, I got Nick hooked. He would call me, and we'd talk about the show. Well, not only the show but Nick's player life too.

The next day, apparently, they had spoken about it. Nick pretty much told me I made myself look like wifey material. Judas was apparently impressed with me.

Not only were we together on the weekend, but we quickly started to spend weeknights together too. I'd come over after work so much that it just made more sense to spend the night with packed work clothes. In time, my toothbrush would be left. Eventually, my razor and panties would get left too.

It was so cute when I wanted to wash my hair for the first time but couldn't find the shampoo. That was because he didn't have any. He had an all-in-one guy body wash and shampoo combo, which didn't make sense to me... but whatever. The next day after work, there was an Argon Oil

Shampoo and Conditioner left for me in the shower. So thoughtful, right? It was particularly special because it had argon oil in it. How did he know?! I was too tickled. Nonetheless, I appreciated his considerate gesture.

Me being at his house practically every single day turned into the normal routine. We'd go grocery shopping. I'd cook. He would go to the liquor store. He'd take the trash out. Kill spiders. He taught me how to use the dishwasher. He said that it was "very non-American of me to not know how to use the dishwasher, yet he wasn't surprised whatsoever that I was completely clueless." Lol.

CHAPTER 5

On Sundays, when he'd go to work in the morning, I'd do laundry.

We were together so much that we even took showers together practically every day. It almost felt weird when I didn't shower with him. Admittingly, I'd wait until he came back from work so we could shower together. We always lotioned each other and massaged one another. We had passionate sex regularly-- very regularly I might add.

During the time we spend together, there were actual conversations, TV watching, laughter, and cuddling.

We talked about a wide variety of topics:

1. How we meshed so well together
2. His daughter whom he loved to the moon and back
3. Our childhood and our parents
4. His mom retiring and traveling back to Trinidad and NY regularly
5. His family in Trinidad and in Panama
6. Our friends
7. His dreams and goals
8. How our kids would be. We both swore our genes were the strongest ones. He was adamant our kids (at least the 1st one) would look exactly like him... smh. Whatever. I told him I wanted a son. His response, "I got chu." Smdh.
9. Current events
10. Our beliefs as Christians (Yes, Jesus Followers who had sex and drank)
11. Sports and ratchet TV
12. His graduation finally arriving

And much more...

Remember, Judas had his daughter when he first started school. So, he delayed his education and took it slow. He worked super hard to provide for his daughter. Oh, how he would talk about her. His pride and joy.

Anyways, it took him like 8-9 years to finish undergrad, amongst the multiple changes he made with his major as well. He even studied nursing for a while, which through me off completely.

Despite the challenges, today was the big day, and he practically invited the entire Meetup Group downtown to the University's ceremony. Some showed up, and you already know I was there. I was so proud of him, his drive, and his determination. The boy graduated with honors too!

I got him a graduation card and a bottle to celebrate later on. I also sent him a nice little photo of me while we were waiting for the ceremony to begin. You see, the night before, I decided to take an erotic pic (if you know what I mean) so that I could send it to Judas. I had never done it before and thought it would be a sexy gesture. I watched him pull out his phone under his graduation gown, look at my photo, and then his phone took a tumble. Yes, he dropped his phone! I figured that meant he liked it. Lol. Some may call it sending my pussy through the mail, but eh.

Once me and the Meetup Group finally found him after the ceremony, you could tell he was happy. As you can imagine, the crowd was a nightmare, so he had to leave us (and me) to find his mom. If y'all know anything about immigrant parents, finding them in situations like these could take F-O-R-E-V-E-R!

So, I let him go and told him we'd meet up later.

Later that night, everyone wanted to celebrate his win. So, we all went out and had a blast! Judas even told me he loved me. Yeah, IKR. IDK if it was the drinks or what. You know some people say babies and drunks tell the truth, but drunks can just be talking and not know what they are saying either... right?? Well, because I couldn't decide if it was genuinely a cause for concern, I ignored it. Truthfully, that wasn't the first time. That was the 2ⁿᵈ time he told me he loved me, but again, I left it alone since he had been drinking heavily.

According to the blog "Do People Actually Tell The Truth When Drunk" by Anaheim Lighthouse, drunk people actually say a lot more than people think:

"Science tells us a lot about how and why alcohol affects the brain. For example, lowered inhibitions make a person more likely to say what's on their mind. And with lowered social rationalization, they are less able to stop themselves if they haven't said something in the past because they are afraid of what you might think or how you might feel. This is why many people talk very openly about things that are important to them or about secrets when they are drunk. In combination with the social factor of increased attention-seeking, where many people tell you things to show off or to keep your attention, and drunks often overshare or share personal and insightful information.

However, it doesn't necessarily have to be true.

Inhibited emotional processing means that a person is more likely to respond emotionally. If a person is very drunk and feels that they are being attacked or hurt, they are likely to respond extremely aggressively. This can include blatant lying as the brain uses anything it can as a defense mechanism. This is especially true for addicted individuals who are in self-denial because they are in a state where they can easily grasp at anything and tell a half-truth to defend themselves. So, if someone is saying something that seems to exonerate them or put the blame on someone else, or even suggests that they aren't drinking much, it's likely a blatant falsehood.

How can you tell the difference? Sometimes, context matters. Very drunk people often don't have the rationalization skills to be manipulative, so positive emotions and heartfelt conversations are often genuine. If they're speaking and they're angry or defending themselves, it could go either way."

CHAPTER 6

More months went by of the same, non-boring routine. Work, his house, cooking, laundry, chilling, drinking, lots of sex, and QT basically happened almost every single day now. I would literally only go home to get more clothes, and that was it. It was like we were living together. That went on for like 7 months. I still can't believe that.

It was new territory for me personally but not for him. He told me he had lived with a couple of his past girlfriends, and his most recent ex had a son that lived with them full-time. Judas mentioned that he was raising the boy from when he was 2 years old until he was like 5 years old when they finally broke up. He voiced to me how he would get so upset when the father showed up 2 years later, not paying any child support and demanding to see the boy. With all that talk, it didn't make me question what kind of man he'd be if we had any kids, you know. It took a special kind of man to be a father, but a whole 'nother kind of special to be a father for the fatherless.

.

.

.

So it was finally the end of September, which meant one thing: Judas's 31st birthday!

I wanted to surprise him with something ...small. I thought it would be a fantastic idea to get an individual bottle of liquor that he would find at his doorstep when he got home. I texted him to see if he was home, and he wasn't. So that was perfect. I put the bottle in a birthday bag, slipped in a birthday card, and headed for his apartment.

When I got there, the garage gate was already opened. Good thing too, because I completely forgot I needed to be buzzed in to park. I usually just walked inside the building from the garage since that door was rarely ever locked. So, I walked in, left the gift at his door, and hoped no one would steal it.

Like I said, I knew he wasn't home per his texts. Therefore, when he came home from a long day, he'd have something to sip on. Sweet of me, right? I thought so.

Later that evening, I received a text from Judas thanking me and telling me he appreciated the surprise. ☺

The next day, it was Saturday and time to celebrate!

We, of course, had the pregame in his clubhouse, and everyone paid a portion for the section at the club. Now, as I'm sure y'all know, you have to get to the section at a certain time. Thus, the pregame had to be quick. Essentially, we all went hard at that pregame, taking shot, after shot, after shot!

He drank. He smoked the hookah. Then, he drank some more! By the end of the night, with all that drinking and burning calories on the dance floor, we were STARVING.

Cookout it was! We needed something heavy to soak up some of the alcohol.

We pretty much rolled up in there 20 deep at like 3:30 a.m. You can only imagine us in line ordering, eating each other's food, and yelling when we thought our volumes were within normal ranges. Aah, good times...

Y'all know what comes after that, right?! Go home, pass out, have sex, and pass out again. LOL.

It was weird though; I mean we could all tell Judas was drunk. The drunkest I had ever seen him. But that wasn't the weird part, though. The part that was out of the ordinary was when multiple people came to me, asking, "You got him?" "You're making sure he gets home?"....etc. Ummm yeah, but how did they know all that??

OMG! Did they know?!? Did he say something to more people?!? I know I HAD to have had a stumped look on my face. I had that, like, I got caught kind of look.

I just nodded, requested the car service, and went back to his apartment.

But for real, was it obvious?

A few days after everyone bounced back to good hydrated health, I had a chat with my homegirl, Shanelle. It was time to spill the tea.

Me: "Sooo, I have something to tell you."

Shanelle: "Ooo, what?"

Me: "But it's a secret."

Shanelle: "Oook, tell me! Tell me!"

Me: "Wellll, you know Judas, right?"

Shanelle: "Mmmm hmmm.."

Me: "Wellll.... we've been talking and hanging out for some months now."

Shanelle: "Aah! Brantley knew something was going on between y'all!"

Me: "He did?!?"

Shanelle: "Yeah girl, he pointed it out to me. The way y'all interact makes it real obvious that y'all are heavy into each other. I'm happy for you. You know when we first met that day, he came up to me asking about you."

Me: "Huh!? Why didn't you tell me?"

Shanelle: "Well, you were with Mike at the time, remember?"

Me: "Oh yeah...hmm, that lying ass nigga."

Shanelle: "Mmmm hm, him."

Me: "But still... and I never noticed him until Dave's birthday at the arcade."

Shanelle: "Yeah, y'all are cute together."

CHAPTER 7

Shortly after the graduation party, I found myself unemployed. Yes, I said the graduation party. And yes, I know that was a while ago.

What had happened was... I was working a contract recruiter position that promised me a permanent position. They took all my commission and used it towards the house account for that branch office. AND to be the top recruiter on the team, that was a lot of money I never received.

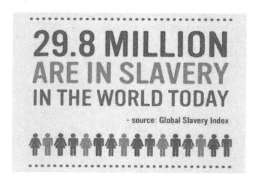

**Welcome to the job.
You have the right to work long
hours for low wages and no
benefits.**

All the above...

Naturally, I became bitter and didn't care to hide it. After I staffed for their national medical account, I was laid off without cause provided. I highly doubt it was a coincidence that they decided to term me the very next morning after speaking to HR about the false promises, sexual harassment attempt, and them forging signatures on consent forms.

I didn't want to tell Judas, but he could tell something was up, so I fessed up... like 3 weeks later.

He was in disbelief but not more than I was! He was all like, "Why didn't you come to me first?"

Probably anger, shame, etc.... duh, I thought to myself. Being unemployed made me feel unworthy and uneasy. I only had a few thousand saved up from my car accident settlement a few years prior.

Deep sigh....

CHAPTER 8

We continued to party but not every single weekend with everyone.

I was still unemployed, so I'd look for jobs at home and go over to Judas's house once he was home. It felt kind of weird not being with him every day anymore. At the same time, I needed to focus, interview, and land a job.

Then after like a month and a half, God blessed me with a job!

Even though it was a contract to hire position, I was so thankful. Funny thing was I had just told myself that I would never settle for a contract to hire position ever again. Nevertheless, it was a job, a check, and not to mention, the others on my team all started as contractors. More than half were already permanent after 3 months; which made me hopeful.

I, of course, told Judas and we had our own celebration.

It was obvious he was happy for me and that he missed how things used to be on a daily basis.

How did I know, you ask?

Well, he'd:

1. Suddenly got jealous when he witnessed other men approach me.

For example, one night, we were out with the group, and I was at the bar waiting for him to come from the bathroom. Then this other guy approached me and sparked conversation. The next thing I knew, he came up behind me, grabbed my waist, and physically got between dude and me to kiss me like he was claiming his territory. It was so obvious that Nick even said something.

2. Shared old pics of our time spent together.

There were times when he'd be at work while I'd be job hunting at home, and he'd send me old selfies he took of us during our excursions in the streets. Studies have shown that people who reminisce about the past tend to be missing those good times, and "gives us the warm and fuzzies."

3. Told me random things he saw that reminded him of us or me.

Remember, I told you that he worked at that international furniture retail store. Well, when he would walk the floors, he'd see a plethora of people who could literally spend all day looking at displays and writing item numbers on their cards for purchase. There was an Asian couple holding hands one day, and for some reason or another, that made him "think of me," per his text.

4. Initiated texts saying, "I miss you."

Self-explanatory.

5. Insistent on seeing me and not just for sex either.

When I was job searching, I wouldn't see him every day like I had been doing. Mainly because I was focused on securing a job, but also because being unemployed didn't make me feel like the perfect package. You know, it made me feel less than and somehow less attractive.

Nonetheless, it didn't seem to bother him. He'd insist I come over, or vice versa, so we could spend time together. Believe it or not, we didn't always have sex—regardless of whether I was menstruating or not.

Those are all signs he missed me. Wouldn't you agree??

Well, anywho, all those things convinced me he missed me. Not to mention his throw down when he gave me some celebratory dick upon my job offer.

What?! IJS...

Shortly after, he knew my birthday was in a week and had asked me what I wanted to do.

I obviously wanted to have an epic night with everyone, but I told him maybe next year since I hadn't even started my new job yet.

Do you know what he did next? He made history by:

1. Judas was literally the first guy who stuck around.
2. He was the first one who wanted to celebrate me.
3. He was the first one who wanted to spend my birthday with me.
4. He was also the first one to offer to give me money and sponsor my birthday festivities.

All other guys that I've talked to, dated, or been in a relationship with stopped talking to me or made excuses and broke up with me by this time. Logically, it was like they didn't think I was worth it enough to acknowledge or spend the efforts, time, and money on me.

So, when he told me that, I started tearing up because I was literally in shock. I was speechless. Just his offer made me feel..... loved and cherished, you know? I was worth it enough to someone other than my daddy. Lol.

I thanked him but told him he didn't have to do all that. He insisted and said, "I know how much birthdays mean to you. And I want to do it for you. I got you."

Obviously, he definitely got the business that night.

My birthday eventually came around, and I purposefully stayed under the budget he gave me (minus the Patron bottles). I didn't want to be nor look greedy when he was doing something nice for me.

I had my own bottle of Patron and drank like ¾ of the bottle before we even left the house. IKR!

Needless to say, I was super drunk by the time we got into the car and even more so when we arrived at the destination. Really, really, really, drunk!

I had a good time.... Until the next day.

He went to work, per usual, and I was at the house with liquor poisoning trying to recuperate. Like, I could not hold anything down. Not water, not bread, not ANYTHING! I was throwing up everything y'all! I vomited so much and so hard that I'd even peed on myself. My body was literally like wtf is going on and couldn't function properly. Y'all it was THE WORST. You hear me, THE MOST, ABSOLUTE WORST!!!

Never again, I told myself.

When Judas finally came home from work, I was lying on the floor and probably smelled horrible. I was so exhausted and hungry at the same damn time. I told him what was going on, and I think he thought I was pregnant or something by his reaction.

To ease his mind, I quickly mentioned I thought I had liquor poisoning.

.

.

.

So, remember I said never again? Well, that "never again" arose the next weekend with the Meetup group. I couldn't miss the good times.

This time was different, though.

Although we all met at Judas's to pregame, Judas rode in the car with someone else. A woman. Admittingly, I initially felt a way but brushed it off since we were all cool. So, I rode with Nick instead.

At the club, Judas wasn't all up on me like he normally was either. I just brushed it off again.

BUT THEN we all went to that late-night Chinese restaurant, and Judas still rode in the car with ole' girl. By that point, I started to feel a way for sure.

Nick was headed out and offered me a ride to my car. "Why wouldn't Judas come too since my car and stuff are at his house?" I asked Nick. He kept trying to brush it off and dismiss me. So, I started feeling like Nick was playing games as if he was trying to be a wingman, and I was cock-blocking Judas.

I wasn't having it, so I got in ole' girl's car to take *US* back to Judas's house. When we got outside the complex, she must have thought I was asleep or drunk because she whispered to Judas, "So I guess I can't come in now."

WTF, I said to myself.

Judas: "No, she's drunk. And what am I going to do?"

We got out of the car and walked into the house without exchanging any words. No cuddling and definitely no sex!

The next day, we didn't talk about it. I just went home to process what just happened. I mean... he wasn't my man *officially* but was I really not worth any respect and common courtesy to not try and talk to and/or fuck a girl we both know from the Meetup group?! Or was I overacting because he's single and wasn't mine to claim? OR was I totally justified in feeling a way? And what way was that exactly? That I could be into him more than I realized? That I wanted him to be mine exclusively??

I took a break from Judas to process what had happened and to gather my feelings. He was texting me, but I was short with him IF I even responded for those days. I just needed some time.

.

.

.

Eventually, he wanted me to come over and have a discussion. So, I went over there... the day *after* he suggested.

He apologized and said it wouldn't happen again. "It" meaning the disrespect-- intentional or not. He SAID, "I don't want that bitch, and we never had a romantic relationship." Romantic relationship as in fucked and oral. IDK that I believed it 100%, but I accepted his apology. I told myself I would proceed with caution and be more mindful just in case I was blinded like before.

CHAPTER 9:

We continued to date, but it wasn't every day, all day, outside of work anymore. It was just most of the time. Like, maybe 5-6 days a week instead of the full 7.

I slowly stopped the constant cooking and putting his clothes away. He would have to re-earn those privileges.

During those times, he expressed more of his woes. He was doing well at work but felt like he wanted more official responsibility.... and of course... that meant more money.

He had started with that well-known international furniture retailer as a kitchen showroom, builder person. You know, the ones that assembled the kitchen displays in the store. Then somehow, by God's grace, he became an HR Generalist and had been with that company for 9 years without having completed his bachelor's until this past summer. From what he expressed, he was the go-to person before the Director, and the Director relied on him as well. However, the issue was that he didn't have a higher title. The next level for him was his boss's position, and she was not going anywhere anytime soon. So, we decided another company would be more beneficial. I had no doubts he'd get another position quickly, especially with his job history with the same company and his advancement.

I also mentioned that he should consider getting his PHR (Professional HR License), which would boost his credentials as well. He had the requirements of over 3 years of experience.

[Sidebar: I only knew that because I just enrolled for the PHR class to take the exam upon course completion. But I didn't mention that to him because:

1. It wasn't about me at the moment

And

2. I didn't want to jinx it, especially if I didn't pass.]

It says something when a man confides in you about his goals. Then, when you put bugs in his ears to pursue something, and he listens... That's a beautiful thing.

Men don't realize how valuable us women are in supporting roles. Without our encouragement, I doubt they'd succeed in life. Seriously.

(

CHAPTER 10:

So, with all that time we've spent together regularly for like 9 months, me feeling a way about him in the car with another woman, and him apologizing to sharing his goals—it got me thinking hard. Hard about what I wanted. After much deliberation, I determined I wanted him. It was the only logical explanation.

As a result, I brought it up. My 2nd time in life bringing up the idea of a relationship.

The 1st time was with Chris in VA, but then he declined and got shipped overseas for a year anyways.

So, my record was 0-1. Not so good.

I was nervous, but I put my big girl panties on anyways.

.

.

.

The next day, I went over there and made dinner, and that was where I brought it up.

Me: "So we've been talking for a while now."

Judas: "Yeah, it'll be a year in March."

Me: "Mm-hmm. And we are together a lot. And I think you like me enough to want to be around me constantly, we mesh well, understand each other, have great chemistry and sex...etc. And we kinda act like we are in a relationship..."

Judas: "Mm-hmm."

Me: "Wouldn't you agree?"

Judas: "I mean well.... Yes, we do mesh well, and if I was in that headspace, then I would definitely wife you up. BUT I am just focused on getting a new job for the new year and not on a committed monogamous relationship right now. Once I get a new job, then the focus will change, and we can talk about a relationship then...?"

Me: "Oh, I see."

I was bummed but appreciated his honesty. I also understood that when a man is focused on something, nothing else matters until he accomplishes that particular thing. I understood, let it go, and didn't bring it up any further.

My record was now 0-2.

Naturally, I fell back some more. Didn't spend as much time with him, per the usual. The original, usual. Maybe like 3-4 times a week instead of 5-6 times per week.

He wanted to focus on getting a new job, soooo I let him.

A couple of weeks later, he broke the news to me.

Judas: "I got the job!"

Me: "That's awesome, congrats! I knew you would, and I was praying for you!"

Judas: "Thank you. Everyone was praying for me."

Me: "Everyone??"

Judas (laughing): "Yeah... you... my mom..... everyone."

Me: "Ha, so I guess we are everyone then. We will have to do something to celebrate. My treat!"

Judas: "No, that's ok. I don't want you to spend any money on me."

Me: "Hmmm, ok..."

I thought that was weird. Who turns down a celebratory dinner? Especially from someone they've spent so much time with.

IDK... I just didn't say anything else about it and left it at the "hmmm ok."

We had dinner, watched TV, and had sex, per usual. I went home the next morning and just handled other matters.

I didn't see him for a few days but received a text that he was at STK with another woman. She was from the Meetup, so I figured maybe a group of them was there. Turned out, it was just them 2.

Interesting, huh?

That was someone I invited over to my home to include in girl's night and everything. At the moment, it was gossip, but since I knew Bethany, I just reached out to her directly to meet up for sushi.

I thought it would be more mature and womanlier to just have a woman to woman conversation to get the facts. I have never fought over a man, EVER, and don't ever intend to; unless it was my daddy or future son(s). Otherwise, I would let a nigga go, no matter how attached I may feel.

I also invited another friend, Karen, but told her to come 30 minutes after our conversation. That was so it wouldn't seem like Bethany was being ambushed because that wasn't the intent whatsoever.

My intent was legitimately to have a mature conversation and get her side before I went to Judas.

A few days later, we met up at the sushi spot in Midtown.

Me: "So, I wanted to talk to you about something."

Her: "Ok."

Me: "I was told you and Judas were at a steakhouse the other day?"

Her: "Yeah, celebrating his new job!"

Me: "Oh..ok.."

I started feeling a way. An even *bigger* way.

Me: "I don't think it's a secret anymore that Judas and I are talking. But at the end of the day, he isn't mine to claim. So, I am just wondering if y'all are talking/dating or romantically involved on any level? Just so you know too, it's not because I am putting a claim on him or anything. So please don't think that. I just need to know the facts, because if so, then I will fall back completely and let y'all do y'alls thing...?"

Her: "Ummmm, no. We are just friends. We haven't had sex or kissed or anything."

Me: "Ok. I mean it's ok if y'all are. Like I said, I will fall back. But I wanted to have the discussion with you directly."

Her: "No, I don't want him, girl."

Me: "Ok, now that that's out of the way, I also invited Karen. She should be here soon. I told her she could join us but gave her a later time so you wouldn't feel like this was a setup."

Her: "Ok, cool. I like Karen."

Sooo. I was giving her the benefit of the doubt because:

1. Her intent *could* just be friends.
2. Men lie.
3. That could be Judas trying to get out of the friend zone with her.

4. Why would *SHE* lie as a woman? Especially if I told her I'd fall way back completely to let her have him without me as a distraction of any sort?

Well, minutes later, Karen joined us. Dinner seemed normal to me.

By then, my rage shifted from 50% to 100% towards Judas. So, the next day I went to Judas's house.

I walked in and took off my shoes while he was the computer. I stood in the kitchen and without any hellos, went in on him.

Me: "You wanna talk about this now or later?"

Him: "Ummm, later?"

Me: "Wrong answer."

Him: "So why did you ask me?"

Me: "It was rhetorical... so your date with Bethany the other day..."

Him: "Yeah, she told me about how you and Karen set her up yesterday, and you were putting a claim on me."

Me: "Excuse me?!?"

I was totally shocked y'all.

Me: "I literally said verbatim, 'I am not putting a claim on him, and if y'all are talking, let me know, and I will fall back.'"

Him: "Why didn't you just ask me? We are just friends."

Me: "I just did."

Him: "Why even get her involved? What was your purpose for that?"

Me: "As a woman, I wanted to hear her side and listen to yours too. But sounds like either both of you are lying or just one of you."

Him: "Well, it's not me."

Me: "Mm-hmm...We already had this conversation. I know we are not official, but that's completely disrespectful to be seen on a date with someone I've hung out with outside of you. Period!"

Him: "You're right. We did talk about that. I am not interested in a relationship right now."

Me: "You said your focus was on getting a new job. And you've done that now. And we already act like we are in one. So why not just make it official and be in a committed monogamous relationship?"

Him: "I just want to have fun. No commitments. I realized I've always been in a relationship, and right now, I don't want that commitment."

Me: "Ok, so you 'finding a job as your focus' was just you stalling, pretty much?"

Him: "Nooo..."

Me: "Mm-hmm..."

I cut him off before he could try to BS me anymore.

I grabbed my toothbrush, razor, and clothes then stormed out.

He didn't try to stop me, nor send me a text after that. Nothing!

I guess that was it.

CHAPTER 11:

So, I went home extra smad (sad + mad). Unwanted. Unworthy. Could it be because I was just not good enough? Why waste all that time if you knew you didn't want anything serious yet suggested otherwise? I didn't get it.

Each day went by, and it still felt weird to not be around him. Watching TV, cooking for 1, showering by myself, and sleeping alone was awkward.

I mean, don't be fooled. Niggas was always texting me and trying to spend time with me. I personally just didn't have sex with more than 1 person at a time. I don't even kiss more than 1 person at a time. I don't judge anyone who does.... In fact, I can't even think of 1 friend who didn't besides me.

Well, anyway, it was weird.

I wanted to text him because he was obviously on my mind and I missed him... but I didn't. I promise!

.

.

.

What felt like ages only turned out to be an entire week and a half.

I got a text saying, "Have a good first day. I miss you." from none other than Judas himself.

I didn't respond immediately, but rather thunk on it (as they say in the South).

After a few hours of not responding, he sent another message to ask if we were still going to my friend's sister's traditional Nigerian wedding together that coming weekend.

Shoot! That's right, it was that weekend. Somehow (yes somehow) I admitted I missed him too.

I know! I know!

I repeat IDK what happened! My fingers had a mind of their own I tell ya! Honest!

So, we continued to text throughout the week, but I didn't go over there for any sleepovers.

He flat out told me he didn't want to be in a relationship, and I had no choice but to accept that and not expect it to change.

I did, however, go over there earlier on Saturday because my other friend was also having a birthday party at this place in Midtown. So, we had 2 places we had to go to.

But 1st, the wedding which started at 7:00 p.m.

The venue was out in the middle of nowhere, and I thought we were late because it was already 7:30 p.m.!

Turns out, we were early. Yes, early y'all!

NO ONE told me there was a such thing as Nigerian Time. You know, like, CP Time but waaaaay worse! We got there at 7:30 p.m., yet the invitation said the ceremony began at 7:00 p.m.

There was hardly anyone there yet either. People SLOWLY started to arrive with their traditional garments, but the ceremony did not even begin until like 10:30 p.m. Yes, 10:30 p.m.!! 3 hours later!

So, Judas and I indulged in the open bar. Even still, that was a long wait. Remember, we still had to make it back to the city for the birthday party too. Ugh. I was low key frustrated, but Judas wasn't—at least I couldn't tell otherwise.

To sum up, we could only stay for an hour because the wedding was 3 hours later than I had anticipated. Correction: later than I was told, not just anticipated.

I had a good ass buzz, but I was STARVING. Luckily, Judas and I found a Popeye's and got food. We ate it on the way to the birthday party.

Our vibes, you ask?

Well, the vibes were fine. Like nothing had ever happened, which kind of confused me. Nonetheless, the vibes were good.

We finally made it to civilization 40 minutes later, so obviously, my buzz was practically gone. Thankfully, Krystal had a section, so we took shots the moment we arrived. It was a small party. Krystal and her man at the time, Shanelle and her man Brantley, and this other couple that I didn't know. I was grateful Judas was there with me. Otherwise, I'd be the odd woman out.

Now, I've never mentioned this before, but something would always happen when Brantley and Judas got together. It was like they had an instant bromance and almost forgot Shanelle and I even existed. They were like twins, and it didn't help that they both wore the same exact outfit: black suits with the white button-up and skinny black tie. They had the same haircut too. It was ridiculous, yet hilarious at the same damn time.

That was also the first time we did a "couples" thing with *my* friends. So naturally, I got pulled aside by the girls to tell me they liked Judas and how cute our interactions and chemistry was. *Yep, I THOUGHT so too*, I said to myself. I hadn't told them he didn't want a relationship though.

Meanwhile, the "twins" were on the dance floor having a dance battle. SMDH. Instinctively, Shanelle and I recorded them to show off tomorrow. Hehe.

About an hour later, it was time to go. We said our goodbyes and walked back to the car hand in hand. While we were walking, a pigeon was banging its head on the streetlight pole. I, of course, stopped in my tracks in fear because well... birds are freaking scary!

[Sidenote: I feel like birds have no peripheral vision like children? They just be flying and could care less about your head, or your life for that matter—forcing you to dunk every time they fly near you. Looking like a crazy person in the parking lot. Then it didn't help my fear when I saw a bachelorette get "bird-brained". She was drunk and poked her head out of the sunroof of the limo, and then a bird flew in her mouth. ...She died. Exactly! It was from an episode on 1,000 Ways to Die. So now you see why I think birds are scary. It's for good reason.]

Well, anyway, Judas knew I was terrified and kicked the bird out of my path.

Me: "OMG! Is it dead?!?"

Him: "It's not moving. See, I love you so much that I killed a bird for you. These are the times I wished we were in Vegas so we could get married this late at night, and I'd wake up next to you as my wife."

Me in shock ......

I heard some footsteps coming, which was an opener for me to distract his most recent comment on marriage.

Me: "Ok, let's go before someone notices."

We walked another block back towards the car.

Aaah, we made it... I thought to myself.

That night we had sex like never before. A more passionate kind of sex. IDK. The man told me he loved me for the 3rd or 4th time now. He killed a bird to "save me because he loved me that much."

Was the alcohol to blame for him saying that? OR did he truly mean it in his heart?

Deep sigh... IDK!!

I left the next morning with some random excuse. The truth was I wanted to avoid him telling me he loved me again and to process everything since he also said he didn't want a relationship.

A week went by, and the group chat was talking about Dave's upcoming birthday. IDK if y'all can recall, but that is where Judas and I first met. I couldn't believe an entire year had gone by.

I want to say that I initiated the "I miss you" text that time and suggested we go together. He agreed that I'd meet him at his place that Friday night.

As soon as I walked into the door, Judas threw himself at me. Literally. Then bent me over the chair and well.... handled me. Lol.

Was it me, or was he giving mixed signals?

I only allowed it to be a quickie so I could wash off and take a couple of shots before we headed out.

He requested the car, and we made it to the party that was like 5 minutes away.

Judas opened the door, took my hand, and walked inside to see everyone. It was more of a pale venue, so naturally they had already started to end their night....if you catch my drift. That venue had games like pool and life-sized tumbling tower blocks. There was a bar, of course, and seating for lounging and eating.

Shortly after our arrival, Dave wanted to sit and eat. So, I sat and waited for Judas.

I'm sure they noticed we walked in hand in hand. Then, when he brought me a drink and sat right next to me, I could see them lurking. It later became clear they knew about us.

Anyways, we called it a night after some drinks and headed back to his apartment.

We finished what he had started before we left the house.

Once we were done, he spooned me and whispered in my ear, "I love you."

Yes, AGAIN! I knew I was going to have to address it in the morning.

.

.

.

The morning came a few hours later, but his dick woke me up along with him verbally telling me, "Happy Anniversary." Yes, y'all. He remembered and brought it up himself. I had honestly forgotten by that point, but it was a shock *he* remembered. You know, considering that he was someone who didn't want a relationship and all.

I didn't know what to make of it, so I just had sex with him yet again. By that point, it was like round 4.

Afterward, we took a shower. Soooo that was the moment. I guess.

Me: "Sooo..."

Judas: "Yeah, can you believe we've been talking for a whole year?"

Me: "Nope, it went by so fast."

Judas: "Mm-hmm."

Me: "So last night, you told me you loved me."

Judas: "Huh??"

Me: "Yeah."

Judas: "Oh. Well, I was just drunk talking probably."

Me: "Yeah, soo, that wasn't the first time you've said it."

Judas: "It wasn't?!"

Me: "No, it's like the 4th time now."

Judas: "And you're just now telling me this?"

Me: "Yeah. Like you said, I thought it was the alcohol talking, but it keeps happening. And remember when you killed that bird for me? You said it then too. AND added on that you wished we were in Vegas so we could get married because you want to wake up next to me as your wife."

Him: "Are you sure you just weren't hearing things? Because I don't remember any of what you're saying."

Me: "Yes, you said all that."

Him: "Well, I was just drunk then."

With that, he walked out of the shower.

Hmm, ok. He's denying it and/or didn't remember. OR was it really just him not realizing what he was saying?

I thought to myself. And he STILL didn't mention a relationship.

I got out the shower, got dressed, and left—but not before a long kiss goodbye. We both kissed each other like it was going to be the last time.

And it was.

He didn't reach out to me, and I didn't reach out to him.

CHAPTER 12:

Y'all know how it is. When you stop seeing boo, you go back to doing other things. For instance, you return to working out, playing volleyball, and spending more time with friends. With your better friends you always pick up where you left off.

Since women love to eat, sip, and chat, I spent more time brunching with the girls.

I don't know where y'all live, but here in Atlanta, there are literally hundreds of brunch spots. Now, what's brunch without mimosas? Not brunch at all if you ask me.

Although Einstein's didn't have a breakfast buffet, Shanelle, Chris, and I decided to meet there on Juniper. The Gays always brought the entertainment, and Juniper was the place to be for that. They just brought life with every head turn! You could literally pick up a napkin and look back up to see gay pride everywhere. This was a super gay-friendly neighborhood and so much fun!

[Sidenote: Y'all remember my friends Chris and Shanelle? The ones always down for the cause.? Chris is the white girl, and Shanelle is the one from Charlotte, remember?]

Well, anyways, I naturally ordered the mimosa before I even looked at the menu. I mean... duh!

I didn't even notice, but an hour and a half had already gone by when we were ready to collect our checks and go to the next spot. Shanelle pointed out that I didn't even touch my mimosa. IKR! It was unheard of. I must have been mad hungry or something. When I went to gulp it down, it didn't taste right for whatever reason. The juice was sour or something, so I just left it. I figured I'd just catch up at the next spot.

It was such a nice day outside. The sun was shining brightly, and it wasn't scorching per the usual weather for Atlanta. Typically, Atlanta is known for its hot, dry air. My hair and skin were not used to all this southern climate— dry all the time, horrible air quality, and no ocean breeze. Just some nasty brown river water my black American ancestors were enslaved to be around.

But I digress...

It was a sundress kind of day without panties nor booty sweat. Y'all know what I'm talking about. Just perfect for soaking up drinks and some vitamin D.

Amongst catching up, I revealed to them that Judas and I had stopped talking. They were shocked.

Me: "So I haven't seen Judas in a while."

Shanelle: "What's a while?"

Me: "IDK, a month or so..."

Shanelle: "Oh, wow...what happened?"

Me: "Well, a combination of things. First, he told me he wanted to get a new job before entering into a real relationship—an actual committed monogamous relationship."

Shanelle: "Well, when a man has a goal, they can only focus on that thing. I read that men are not natural multi-taskers like us women. So they can literally only focus on one thing at a time."

Chris: "True."

Me: "Yeah, that makes sense now that I think about it. And I did give him the benefit of the doubt. Especially since a man and his job is like a man and his dog. I feel like they go hand in hand...So I encouraged him to pursue his PHR, well really his SPHR, but whatever. At the end of the day, that nigga received an offer that he ultimately accepted."

Chris: "That's good!"

Me: "Yeah, it is. Except when I was like, 'So you got your new job. Let's celebrate-- my treat' and he turned it down because I 'just started my new job after being out of work for a couple months.'"

Chris: "That's considerate."

Shanelle: "Mmm idk..."

Me: "Well, I originally thought it was considerate UNTIL I had to call him out because he was spotted at the Steakhouse with ole' girl... and only with ole' girl!"

"Yes! So, after I called him out in person, that's when he decided it was a good time to be honest and mention he just wanted to be single. Free of commitments right now."

Shanelle: "Mm see. I knew something wasn't right. Considerate, humph!"

Chris: "That's immature. See, that's a boy, not a man!"

Me: "Yeah, so he told me he wanted a job first then a relationship. And once he got his job, still no relationship."

Shanelle: "Still no relationship..."

Me: "Mm-hm, so we weren't on the same page, and I got my stuff, like the toothbrush, razor, panties,...etc. and left."

Chris and Shanelle: "Oh..."

Me: "Yeah, but then a couple weeks later, Dave had his birthday party."

Chris: "Oh yeah, that's right, he just had a birthday. I couldn't go."

Shanelle: "What's his birthday have to do with you and this story?!"

Me: "Welllll... somehow, Judas and I went together and had a last hoorah moment. He even said happy anniversary the next morning."

Shanelle: "You didn't?!"

Me: "I did. But it even felt like the last time."

Shanelle: "Like a breakup?"

Me: "Yeah, I suppose..."

Shanelle: "Yeah, because y'all were together ALLLLL the time. Anytime I texted you, you were always at Judas's..."

Me: "You right.... Enough about that. "

Chris: "Yeah- "

Chris proceeds to change the subject.

Somehow, we got on the topic of periods. Either Shanelle said she was crabby with Brantley earlier that week, or Chris said she could feel her period coming on or something. I can't remember exactly. What I do remember is that I mentioned to them I didn't have my period last month for sure and couldn't remember about the month before that. That job hunt had me stressing out of this world, and I've not had my period 2 other times before, so I wasn't tripping.

They looked worried, but I was confidently telling them I wasn't worried at all, nor was I pregnant. No way! I was faithfully taking my birth control at 6:00 p.m. daily. DAILY.

After a while, we parted ways. Our conversation *did* have me thinking, though....

Yes. The following were true:

1. I didn't have my period for almost 2 months.
2. I have missed a period in the past. Actually, twice before.
3. I was unemployed during the missed period, and stress CAN cause a late or missed period.

    According to an online article in Everyday Health and medically reviewed by Bass III, MD, MPH, Pat F, "The female reproductive system can be affected, too. In fact, for some women, stress may play a role in causing irregular or missed periods. As stress levels rise, there's a chance that your menstrual period will temporarily stop, a condition known as secondary amenorrhea."

4. I was popping those birth control pills faithfully per the doctor's orders. Daily.
5. I haven't had sex since Judas, and that was... Hmmm. Almost 2 months ago.

.... Can't be, right?!?!?

Omg! I immediately went straight to the store, and embarrassingly bought an at-home pregnancy test.

CHAPTER 13:

I was too scared to take the test that night. Plus, I don't like to go to bed any other way except with a peaceful and happy spirit.

So, I watched some *Golden Girls* to get my mind off of things. Mostly off of *it*.

BUT....

The next morning, when I woke up for work at 6:30 a.m.- now *that* was an entirely different story. At the same time, I was still pretty confident that I was not pregnant. I just wanted to take the test for my own sanity and prove the girls wrong from their suspicions.

Y'all know the normal routine: wake up, stretch, and urinate. That's when I peed on the stick.

I peed on the stick, gently placed it on the counter, grabbed some toilet paper, and took a glance at the test.

I instantly did a double take because there it was showing 2 lines!!!

I quickly wiped and hopped off the toilet to re-read the instructions.

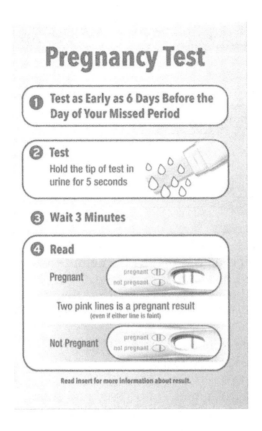

Uh uh. That cannot be right. It can't be! I cannot be pregnant!

OH! EM! GEEEEE!!!!!

In a matter of 45 seconds, I found out I was *allegedly* pregnant and found it harder to breathe with every passing moment.

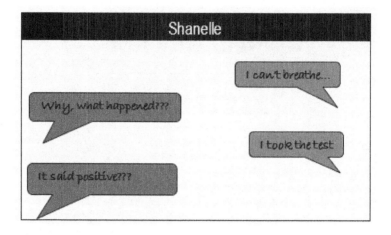

Shanelle

I can't breathe...

Why, what happened???

I took the test

It said positive???

I couldn't even respond with a definite answer because:
1. I didn't want it to be true.
2. The lines showed up so fast that the test could have been defected. Yes, defected. It could happen!

Ok, let me calm down some. That's true, the test could be defected, I said to myself.

I washed my hands, got dressed and stuck the 2nd test in my purse (because you should always buy the 2 pack at minimum). I headed to work, but all I could think about were those alleged test results.

How accurate are those things anyway? I mean, really.

Pregnant. Pregnant! PREGNANT! That's all I heard in my head.

The moment I had to urinate, I took my bag and headed for the restroom. I peed on that stick so hard while praying to God that it would only show one line instead of two this time.

I laid it down, wiped up, and took a look at that thing. Did you know that little shit *still* had two lines on it!?

So naturally, my freak out level went even higher. I had literally never been pregnant before, so *this* level of freak out I didn't even know could exist.

That moment after I could find myself to leave the bathroom, I texted Judas first thing on May 20th, 2015.

Me: "Hey. We need to talk so let me know when you're free this week."

Judas: "What's wrong?"

Me: "Well there's something we need to discuss, and I think an in-person convo is more appropriate."

Him: "Can you talk on the phone now? Because I've got a lot going on this weekend."

Me: "Sorry can't. And you do know I work up the street from your house so it doesn't have to wait until the weekend."

Him: "I might have some time after work but can it wait until next week?"

Me: "It can. Just let me know."

Him: "What time do you get off today? I can be home around 5:30."

Me: "Ok I will be there then."

The remainder of that day, I kept my head down. I didn't talk to anyone except Judas, and the moment I could, I rushed out of there towards Judas's house.

He lived 3 miles from that job, but in Buckhead at that particular time, it took like 30 minutes to get there. He buzzed me in, I parked and then slowly and anxiously walked to his apartment.

I didn't even knock, I just walked in. I know but keep in my mind my brain was on this news. Geesh!

When I walked in, he was on the couch with a drink. I immediately asked him to pour me some water (I didn't

know at the time, but pregnancy makes you extra thirsty).
Anyways, the convo:

Him: "What's up?"

Me: "Soooo, I took a test, and it said positive."

Him: "What test? A pregnancy test?"

Me (avoiding eye contact): "Yeah."

He silently walked from the kitchen to sit back on the couch.

Me: "I just found out this morning. I even took 2 tests."

Him: Silence.

Me: "I'm not sure how far along I am. I researched it, and it said I can take a blood test to find out."

Him: Silence.

Me: "Yeah, so..."

Him: Silence.

Me: "I mean, I've never been pregnant before..."

Waiting for him to say something...*anything* at this point.

Him: Silence.

Me: "Ok, so it doesn't sound like you have anything to say, so I'm just going to leave then."

I did pause before officially grabbing my purse to leave in hopes he'd stop me, but nah, he didn't stop me.

I almost didn't make it to the car before the tears began to stream down my face. I wasn't expecting a marriage proposal or anything like that; HOWEVER, I was expecting an "It'll be ok," "We will get through this," or something! Instead, I got nothing. Literally crickets.

I bawled in the parking garage for about 15-20 minutes. After that, I managed to pull myself together enough to drive home. At that point, the phone rang. It was Judas.

Me: "Hello?"

Him: "Hey, I'm sorry for being so quiet and silent. I am literally speechless and don't know what to say."

Me (Still sniffling from crying): "You act like I've been through this before. I haven't! I am freaking out! This is not *your* first time."

Him: "I know, and I am sorry for my reaction. Do you want to come back and talk?"

Me: "No, I'm almost home, and I'm tired."

I wasn't really almost home. But with the time-lapse and the tears, I didn't want him to see me that way.

Him: "Oh, ok."

Silence.

Me: "So I guess I'll go find out how far along I am and let you know.

Him: "Cool. It'll be ok. We'll get through it."

Me: "Ok. Thanks for calling to apologize."

Him: "Yeah, I didn't' want it to end like that. I was just in shock. I still am."

Me: "Me too. How do you think I feel? And have been feeling all day?"

Him: "I understand. We will figure it out."

Me: "Ok, I'll ttyl."

Him: "Ok, sounds good."

Me: "Bye."

Ok, so that did make me feel a little better. I was glad he called to apologize for his silent reaction. HOWEVER... I was still shocked about this pregnancy news and still with a 10% chance of hope the doctor will tell me it's a false alarm.

Once I got home, I was actually tired. I took a shower and went to bed. Yes, without eating dinner.

CHAPTER 14:

I got into bed but couldn't really sleep. I mean, would you be able to sleep?

It baffled me how I could be pregnant. I know it only takes one time, but I was on birth control! I took it every single day at 6:00 p.m., and we had been sleeping together for an entire year without any pregnancies. It made no sense to me.

I'm sure y'all know where I was coming from, but by the time I could actually fall asleep, it seemed like 5 minutes later, the alarm went off. So annoying!

I got up and went to work. I found myself constantly checking my belly to see if it was noticeable at all. I know, I know. I had just found out yesterday, but I still didn't know how far along I was. Plus, the whole thing was new. I was paranoid. Give me a break!

While I was at work, I was still quiet but trying to remain the same. I was also trying to become less paranoid, but that didn't happen.

IDK if y'all remember, but I was a contractor, not a permanent employee. That alone brought extra stress. The other stressors included:

1. I wasn't married.
2. I literally just turned 26 a few months ago, so I just became ineligible for Tricare and being on my grandparents' insurance. So, I had to apply for Medicaid and see if they'd approve me.
3. Omg! How was I going to tell my grandparents????
4. I didn't make enough money to support a baby and me.
5. As a contractor, I was not entitled to FMLA, PTO, maturity leave, etc. Even if I did go permanent, I

knew pregnancy qualified as a pre-existing condition.

UGH!

I needed a plan.

First things first: I needed to find out how far along I was. Naturally, I internet searched how to find this out. The results: a blood test.

Okay, I needed to find a blood-testing center/clinic and figure out how much it was going to cost.

I researched the closest one that was open on the weekend. Remember, I was an hourly contractor, so, unfortunately, I couldn't afford to miss work.

I found one nearby, called them for the price, and put it on my calendar to go when they first opened Saturday morning.

I let Judas know I was going on Saturday and would keep him updated. Also, we both mentioned we couldn't sleep nor stop thinking about this situation and said nothing else.

Next, I needed prenatal vitamins. I also added that to my to-do list after work.

Ding! Ding! *"What alert did I have going on today?"* I asked myself.

Alert

Volleyball League Game @ 7pm

Crap! I signed up for a volleyball league for Thursday evenings in Buckhead a couple of weeks prior, and we were undefeated. Crap! OMG, I was going to have to quit the league. Ugh! Oooor maybe I could play a few more weeks, depending on how far along I was. Plus, I wasn't showing yet, and balls don't generally fly around aiming for my stomach. I mean, not without me hitting it. I should be alright. At least one last time, then I'll go get those vitamins.

Soooooo... I went to play volleyball but found myself extra cautious. I didn't realize balls were flying around, and I could turn around waiting for our game to start and *Boom!* Get hit directly in the stomach. Oh no, I could feel the anxiety developing. Even though I still ended up playing in the game, I was so paranoid. I didn't play as intensely as I normally would have; as in, I didn't dive. Luckily, no balls flew in my direction that I couldn't protect baby from, which was good. That seemed like the longest game ever, though.

At that point, I knew what I had to do. I emailed them and quit without an explanation. They didn't understand, and I didn't give them any details. I barely knew them but for a few weeks, so it was none of their business. Well, that's how I felt anyway.

Saturday could not have come fast enough. I set my alarm to be at that clinic once they first opened for the day. Since they didn't take appointments, I had it set in my mind that there was going to be a line. IDK about y'all, but I absolutely hated waiting to be serviced.

I got to the clinic like 5 minutes before they opened, so I waited in the parking lot for a bit. IDK if you've noticed or not, but Atlanta has a lot of black people, meaning they will not open them doors even *one minute* before they are due to open for ANY reason whatsoever.

5 minutes normally doesn't seem long when you're a kid asking for 5 more minutes to watch TV before bed, but it sure felt long that day.

I was nervous as hell and didn't know what to expect. Would it be like a doctor's office environment? I had no idea.

Let me tell you, it wasn't a doctor's office kind of scene. No one was there except the girl and me at the front desk. I had to check-in, fill out all kinds of personal information, and pay upfront. She took the payment and told me to hold on because she had to setup.

Me: "Setup?!?"

Ole' Girl: "Yes, I have to get the supplies to draw your blood for the pregnancy test."

Me: "You're the only one here?!?"

Ole' Girl: "Yes."

Me: "OK, sorry. I thought you were a receptionist at the front desk."

Ole' Girl: "We have to do both jobs."

Me: "Oh, I see."

Ole' Girl (chuckling): "Yeap."

I asked myself what have I gotten myself into. If I didn't see gloves and new sterile equipment, I was going to leave.

The Lord heard my thoughts because she came back out with an unopened needle, test tubes, and new gloves. That made me feel a little better. I guess it was a similar setup to the Minute Clinic.

She drew blood and proceeded to tell me that the results would come in about a week.

Me: "A week?!? It's not instant?"

Ole' Girl: "No, only urine tests are instant. To find out how far along you are, we have to send your blood off to a lab for the results.

Me: "Oh, ok. I really thought I'd find out today."

Ole' Girl: "No, we will call you and send you an email with the results."

Ugh, that was annoying! I wanted those results now!! I could be... who knew how many months! Ugh!

I texted Judas to let him know I took the blood test, the results would take like a week, and I'd follow up then. He said, "Ok."

After I left there, I went to pick up some prenatal vitamins. Y'all, there were soo many different kinds. Darn capitalism gives people too many options. They should be like other countries and only supply good quality products for purchase.

This was how my brain was processing:

- *Let me find some prenatals. Hmm...which brand?*
- *Oh yeah, that yellow labeled brand is who I normally buy for vitamins.*
- *Do they even have prenatals?*
- *Aah, they do!*
- *Oh no, 2 different kinds.*
- *This one has added DHA.*
- *Let me research on my phone real quick.*
- *Ok, it said that's something baby needs.*
- *This one with the added DHA it is then.*
- *$20?!?*
- *I guess I have no choice. I wonder if the doctor could prescribe them so the insurance company would have to pay instead of me directly. Hmmm.*

I bought the darn prenatals and took them once I got home.

Once I sat down, thoughts started attacking my mind:

- *I'm not really pregnant, am I?*
- *How am I going to tell Halmoni (Grandma in Korean) and them?*
- *How is she going to react?*
  - *She could be 50% happy to finally be getting a great-grandchild and then 50% upset I'm not married.*
  - *Orr, she could just be 100% unhappy.*
  - *Orr, she could be 100% upset I'm not married.*
- *Omg! How am I going to pay for all that stuff?? I read an article some odd years ago that said parents spend like $250k per kid, easy! And that didn't include daycare and education!*
- *What about insurance for the baby and me?!?*
- *How would Judas and I co-parent?*
  - *We get along fine, so that shouldn't be an issue.*
  - *This wouldn't be his first time having a baby.*
  - *What is his family going to think of me? His mom even?*

Okay, I had to bring it back down. If... IF I was pregnant, the stress would not help the baby. I told myself to remain calm— at least until the results were in before I officially added on to the freak-out monitor, which was at 40%.

I was not going to lie. Over the course of the next week, I drank more water than I had ever drank. Maybe I subconsciously thought it was tequila. IDK.

I also ended up buying the book, *What to Expect When You're Expecting*. I figured I could return it if I didn't really need it.

Let's see what else happened:

- I popped those prenatals daily.

- I had random freak out moments.
- I received concerning texts from Shanelle. I just love her.
- I had more random freak out moments.
- Oh, and I slept, which, according to my research, was normal to be extra thirsty and tired... IF pregnancy was the actual cause.

Finally, a week later, I received an email from the clinic with the results. I opened the attachment and got this:

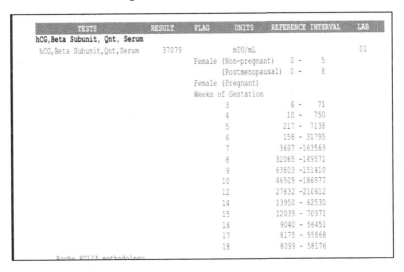

TESTS	RESULT	FLAG	UNITS	REFERENCE INTERVAL	LAB
hCG,Beta Subunit, Qnt, Serum					
hCG,Beta Subunit,Qnt,Serum	37079		mIU/mL		01
		Female (Non-pregnant)		0 - 5	
		(Postmenopausal)		0 - 8	
		Female (Pregnant)			
		Weeks of Gestation			
		3		6 - 71	
		4		10 - 750	
		5		217 - 7138	
		6		158 - 31795	
		7		3697 -163563	
		8		32065 -149571	
		9		63803 -151410	
		10		46509 -186977	
		12		27832 -210612	
		14		13950 - 62530	
		15		12039 - 70971	
		16		9040 - 56451	
		17		8175 - 55868	
		18		8099 - 58176	
Roche ECLIA methodology					

Are you confused AF? So was I. I was totally, completely, and utterly clueless, confused... all the above! Like WTF was this and without an explanation at that.

I mean look at this email:

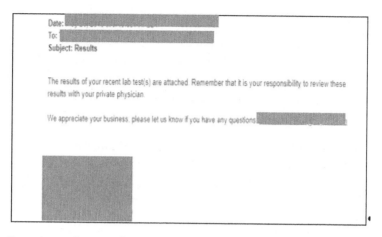

I got nowhere when I tried to call them directly and wanted this shit in *writing*.

After much back and forth without any real answers, I called them yet again. FINALLY, I got someone on the phone—3 days later, I might add.

Apparently, my specific test result number was on the left. I had to find the range I was within, on the right.

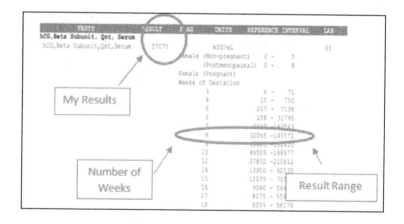

Does that say 8 weeks?!????

Let's try this again, I told myself. So, I relooked at it.

Omg...

Oh, em gee! This was 8 weeks when I took the test a week ago. So technically I was 9 weeks at that point.

Omg! OMG! OMG!!!

I had to take a deep breath. A couple of them actually. I couldn't affect the baby like this. I was sharing this body with baby. Quite literally.

But...

Omg! OMG! OMG!!!

Once I was able to collect myself, I texted Judas to let him know I was around 9 weeks along. Then a couple of days later, I met up with him in person after work.

Judas: "Hey, what's up?"

Me: "Thirsty."

Judas: "Here's some water."

Me: "Thanks."

Judas: "So I've been thinking."

Me: "Uh-huh."

Judas: "I think it would be best to have an abortion."

Me: "Excuse me?"

Him: "Yeah, I mean, I don't want another kid right now. I mean, I'd be ok with more, but I want to have other kids with my wife and someone I actually love and want."

Me: "Mm-hmm."

Him: "Plus, you know, you wouldn't have any support since you're here by yourself, all you have are your grandparents and your mom has M.S."

Me: "Hm."

Him: "And I'd pay for it. The abortion."

Me: "Hm."

Him: "What are your thoughts? I mean, it doesn't make any sense for us to have a baby together."

Me: "Hm."

Him: "How are you feeling about it?"

Me: "Can I get some more water?"

Him: "Yeah."

As he pours another glass...

Me: "Soo... let me get this straight. You want me to get an abortion because you don't want to have any more kids right now. At least not with me?"

Him: "Yeah, I want to get married, or at least love the mother of my future kids."

Me: "Hm... IDK where to begin:

- I thought you grew up Seventh Day Adventist and wouldn't even consider the thought of an abortion?
- Aren't we too old to be having an abortion talk anyways? It's not like we are 16 and pregnant here.
- We don't have to be in a romantic relationship to co-parent and be there for this child."

Him: "I know myself and know how it was with Jasmine's mother. This would only break us apart; Not bring us together as you're hoping."

Me: "What do you mean I don't have support? What about *you*?!?! So I'm not understanding."

Him: "You think my mom is going to raise this kid?!?"

Me: "I didn't say--"

Him (cutting me off): "She's not going to help you! And it sounds like you don't want to have an abortion!"

Me: "Why would I?!? Although I don't judge others who have had them, that is not something I could morally do. Plus, I was on birth control, and the way I see it is that God doesn't make mistakes. He caused this. I feel like--"

Judas (interrupting me again): "Do you think that this will make us be in a relationship?!?"

Me: "I didn't say that—"

Him (cutting me off AGAIN): "You don't have ANY support, and I can't afford another baby! And how could you have been on birth control if you're pregnant now?!?"

My jaw dropped.

Me: "Really, though?!? You witnessed me faithfully taking my pill every day I was here at 6:00 p.m. when the alarm went off. Are you trying to accuse me of fuckin' trappin' you?!?!"

Him: "That doesn't make sense. If you were on birth control, then you wouldn't be pregnant right now."

Me: "How dare you! I didn't just hop on an imaginary dick with your DNA on it, and then tell your sperm to find my egg and fertilize! Not to mention, birth control is not 100% effective!"

Him: "You know what. Sounds like you made up your mind. Don't expect us to get together because of this because I know myself, and I will NOT be there for you or this baby. This will tear us apart. I just know myself."

Me: "Well, if that's how you feel..."

He opened the door. Basically, he non-verbally told me to get the fuck out.

Me: "I don't get that. You know that you're going to hold a grudge, accuse me of trappin' you, be intentionally petty, and not parent this kid as opposed to being mature and co-parenting with me?"

Him: "You don't have a choice at this point!"

Me (storming out): "I do have a choice!"

I walked back to my car with my heart beating so fast from all that just happened. Once I finally got inside, I bawled my eyes out. Who the fuck was that?! On top of that, who the fuck did he think he was?!!

I didn't get it. Why couldn't he be there for us? Us meaning baby and me or at least for baby?

I never implied I wanted to be in a relationship to have this baby. And an abortion?!? And that I trapped him??

I just couldn't believe what just happened and what he just said. He was going to intentionally be petty and vindictive because I didn't want an abortion? He already has a daughter, so this wasn't new for him; this was new for *me*. This meaning getting pregnant.

Can I just say tears were all over the place? I mean, right!?!?

How would you feel if a nigga said all that to you after a year of talking??? And to your pregnant self?

SMDH doesn't begin to express the emotions ...nah, the *pain* that I instantly felt. Pain. Confusion...all the above.

I almost said uncontrolled hormones, but fuck that. I kept my attitude in check. You hear me?! I didn't throw things. I didn't hit. I didn't yell at the top of my lungs. I didn't call him out of his name. I didn't slash his tires on my way back to the car. None of that. I kept my crown on like a queen ought to.

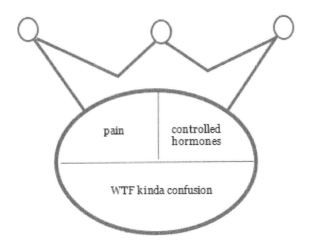

I literally felt kind of lost too. Not like I had lost my marbles or anything, but my emotions were sooo all over the place. I needed to find them and collect myself.

Expressing my feelings was never a strong quality that I possessed, so trying to figure out what I was feeling was challenging. I learned that I was worth expressing my feelings, and it was okay to feel more than one emotion, which was exactly what was going on. My analytical mind was trying to capture a category but couldn't, and *that* was wrecking my brain. I am not the only one, right?

But you know what? For some reason, I started singing "Amazing Grace," and that instantly provided me with comfort. I told baby that was our song to help us calm down and get centered to gather ourselves.

Amazing grace! How sweet the sound
That saved a wretch like me!
I once was lost, but now am found;
Was blind, but now I see.

'Twas grace that taught my heart to fear,
And grace my fears relieved;
How precious did that grace appear
The hour I first believed.

CHAPTER 15:

I had to conjure up a plan....

I thought it would be a good idea to get some advice from 2 single mothers I knew from the Meetup: Natalie and Ciara. I figured I could ask general questions without telling them who the father was.

So, I hit them up and asked flat out: "Do you have any advice for a new single mother?"

Now neither of these ladies were who I'd call friends because I don't use the term "friend" loosely. I will say we knew each other and could hangout without complications. I've been to their homes and vice versa; we both made sure the other got to and from parties okay. I guess some would call that friendly acquaintances. But I can't lie, I did feel like Natalie and I were headed towards an actual friendship.

Ciara responded with a, "Hey girl, it's tough but worth it. Why? Are you pregnant?!?"

Ugh, I had no choice but to tell her yes. It was bound to come out sooner or later.

Ciara: "Yea, it's tough. If you feel nauseous, eat some ginger candy. But rest is very important."

Me: "Thanks for the advice!"

Her: "Does the dad know?"

Me: "Yeah, he does."

Her: "Is he happy, ooor...?"

Me: "Nope, not happy. In fact, he told me flat out to not expect him to be around."

Her: "Wow, that's unfortunate."

Me: "Yeah, it is. I don't get it."

Her: "The same thing happened to me with my first, but he eventually came around. I'm sure the same will happen to you too."

Me: "IDK, I hope so."

.

.

.

I think I forgot to mention that Natalie and Judas were running buddies, so she's the one that revealed he was out with ole' girl celebrating his new job. Naturally, I spoke with her more.

But *anywho...*

I texted Natalie, and she was like, "Oh congrats...does Judas know?" I was like, "What makes you think it's Judas's?"

Natalie: "Really, though?! You know, I know how much time y'all have spent together."

Me: "He hasn't said anything to you about it?"

Her: "No, not yet. But I'll see him tomorrow for a run."

Me: "Oh, ok. Well, he's not happy."

I gave her a brief synopsis that he wasn't fucking with us. She was shocked to hear it and said maybe he was still in shock and would come around.

Me: "Maybe, but that's no excuse."

Her: "You're right. It's not."

Me: "Well, thanks for chatting, but I'm getting sleepy... GN!"

Her: "NP. I'm here if you need anything."

I fell asleep immediately.

Later on, the Meetup chat was blowing up.

Ding! Ding! Ding! Ding! Ding!

They were, in fact, trying to figure out where to go. They wanted to start at a hole in the wall place that had cheap

40 oz beers and a good dance floor. Then to this underground club...literally under the parking lot.

Hmmm, I could use a last night out before shit gets too real, I thought to myself.

That sounded fun, and of course, I wouldn't drink. "Oh, wait," I thought aloud, "Do they smoke in there? Let me ask."

Me (In the group chat): "Do they smoke in there, I can't remember?"

Judas (literally 2 seconds later): "Yes, they do."

My thoughts:

Why the fuck was he responding all swiftly! I wasn't asking *him*, and he just said all those horrible things to me. I'm not speaking to him until he apologizes, explains himself, and then never does it again!

I had a gut feeling he was just trying to make sure I wasn't going because he was out for vengeance.

I wanted to go, but unfortunately (or fortunately; I couldn't decide), I fell asleep again before I could do anything else.

Pregnancy.

Natalie reached out to check on me pretty regularly, though.

Natalie: "Hey girl. How are you feeling?"

Me: "Pretty good. What's up withchu?"

Her: "Just left Judas's."

Me: "Oh, ok."

Her: "He told me you were pregnant."

Me: "Interesting."

Her: "Yeah, were you on birth control?"

Really, this again?, I thought.

Me: "Ummm, that's a weird question. Why?"

Natalie: "Well, if you weren't then that would explain the pregnancy."

Did she just say that? Is she trying to get me to say I fucking trapped that nigga?

Me: "Not to sound defensive, but I'm not sure why we're talking about my birth control. But if you must know, yes, I was."

Her: "Did you take it every day?"

Bish!

Me: "Excuse me?! Where is this headed?"

Her: "Sorry, I'm not trying to offend you, but he brought it up and led me to believe you trapped him."

Me: "I took my pill faithfully every single day up until about 1.5 months ago. He saw me take it when I was over there almost every day for a year."

Her: "A year?!?"

Me: "Yes, a year. So not that I know how to trap someone or would even want to, but if I wanted to trap him, wouldn't I have done it a long ass time ago? From my perspective, he had a deadline that he didn't meet. So I stopped talking to him (AS he did me). We hadn't spoken for 2 months prior to me finding out about the baby."

Her: "What do you mean a deadline?"

116

Me: "If you're talking to someone for almost a year, staying over almost every day and night, cooking, cleaning, laundry, and having sex, eventually you're going to want a relationship. It was already like we were in one anyways."

Her: "Wow, I knew y'all were hanging out, but the way he put it, you were just a jump-off. I didn't know y'all were hanging out like that... that's messed up."

Me: "Exactly! I knew we weren't official, but I also had no idea he was telling people I was a jump-off."

Her: "Same thing happened to me with this one guy."

Me: "Who, Erik?"

Her: "Wait, how'd you know??"

Me: "Girl, you and Erik TRIED to make it a secret, but y'all weren't."

Her: "Well, we were together all the time. I even helped him when he was in transition. He was staying at my house."

Me: "Wait, he was?!? That, I didn't know. So he got ole' girl pregnant when y'all weren't dating then?"

Her: "Wait, how'd you know he was having a baby?"

Me: "Girl, everyone knows that now. I didn't know it was a secret. Is it?"

Her: "I guess not. I'm done with him. He really hurt me, and I loved him so much that I helped pay for some baby stuff like the play pin and stuff."

Me: "Girl!? What!?"

Her: "Yeah, I see now he was just using me. But I couldn't tell because we were always together, and he told me he loved me too.

Me: "Oh wow... I had no idea, especially since I've never seen you guys arrive or leave together at any of the events. So I assumed you wanted y'alls relationship to be kept private. But then, when you blew up at Dave's house about him and another woman, my suspicions were confirmed."

Her: "Yeah, I can't believe I did that. I went from 0-100 real quick."

Me: "Yeah, and Judas has told me he loved me too."

Her: "Did you love him?"

Me: "Love is a strong word. But I had love for him, just not IN love... I never said it back to him."

Her: "Well, I doubt he'd deny that he loved you to me."

Me: "Well IDK. You didn't know we were unofficially shacking up either sooo..."

Her: "No, but we still talked. The only reason I didn't know you were that deep into it was because he was on dates with other women the last few months."

Me: "Interesting... well prior to finding out I was pregnant a couple weeks ago; I/we hadn't spoken since Dave's birthday party in March."

Her: "Oh yea, y'all did show up together. I'm sure he'll come around. He just needs time to calm down."

Me: "He doesn't have any reason(s) to be upset to calm down from. I didn't get pregnant on my own. And this isn't his first, it's mine."

Her: "I'm not disagreeing with you or excusing what he said to you, but he's a guy; they think and process things differently. If he doesn't, then I'll personally say something about it. He'll need to put his big boy draws on and man up."

Me: "Yeah.. well, I'm getting sleepy again."

Her: "NP! I know how it is..."

Natalie continued to check on me regularly, but I still hadn't heard from Judas.

.

.

.

After about a month of texts with Natalie, she was still hopeful Judas would come around and was in disbelief he hadn't yet.

At that point, I was going to all my appointments solo. It was not how I wanted my first pregnancy experience—or any pregnancy experience for that matter—to be. It was sad, embarrassing, upsetting, and unfair that I was alone.

Essentially, here was my daily schedule:

6:30 a.m.: Woke up for work.

8:00 a.m.- 4:57 p.m.: Worked dealing with onboarding retail stores, General Managers, and Regional Managers in multiple states and provinces across the US and Canada.

4:57 p.m. - 5:30 p.m.: Drove in traffic.

5:30 p.m. - who knows: Chilled, ate, watched biblical movies/TV series to keep my spirit up, read the Bible, texted, and eventually fell asleep on the couch.

1:00 a.m. - 3:45 a.m.: Felt nauseous and had to sit up and shower. I watched more biblical shows like Joyce Meyers because it was depressing that I was alone—at least without physical beings in my presence outside of co-workers.

4:00 a.m. – 6:00 a.m.: Slept and woke up for work to do it all over again.

Oh! BTW I did tell my grandparents by way of telling them I wasn't feeling well for a few weeks. Then I gradually told them I eventually went to the doctor and found out I was having a baby.

Surprisingly enough, they were happy for me, yet HIGHLY upset that nigga Judas basically abandoned me. Rightfully so... I mean for them to be angry, not for Judas to have abandoned me.

Now some may think the word "abandon" is harsh. Why, IDK. So, let's define it, shall we?

- Merriam-Webster defines *abandon* as, "To give up with the intent of never again claiming a right or interest in"
- Now, the legal definition says, "intentionally and permanently give up, surrender, leave, desert, or relinquish all interest or ownership in property, a home or other premise, a right of way, and even a spouse, family, or children"

So, let's review so far:

A. Judas and I were talking for a year and practically living together. He had a timeline to make it official but opted against it, so we stopped talking for 2 months.

B. Found out I was pregnant one morning and met up with him that same evening to inform him.

120

C. To sum up: Judas was not happy and was intentionally hurtful and told me he wouldn't be around.

D. I had a job, but it was contract-to-hire and was still in the contracted phase, so Medicaid approved. Thank God!

E. Went to appointments by myself and lived my pregnant life solo—minus God's presence, co-workers, and texts from friends and calls from grandparents.

F. Texted Judas periodically for him to say things such as:

"I already told you I know how I am, so just deal with it." Talking about he will be disrespectful and petty and that I will have to deal with it regardless.

or

"I don't need to talk about you. Get over yourself." Blah blah.

G. I was told that Judas was giving shout outs to his new "bae" on social media, so I mentioned it to Natalie. She wasn't any help.

    a. I decided to get on social media myself to like the post. I wasn't trying to be petty but rather to show support of his new relationship. This way, he wouldn't think I was stuck on him. It was supposed to be like an olive branch to co-parent civilly.

Then I rethought that *like*—to unlike it—and it turned out he blocked me when I went back to unlike it.

H. Literally not a single word from Judas. IDK. In my mind, we didn't have to be in a romantic relationship, but we could've been cool to co-parent, be friends, OR at least be cordial. He could've asked how things were going, checked on our—me and baby's—needs, met me at the appointments, baby shopped, etc. Instead, I got nothing.

Now with all that, if you're not convinced Judas abandoned me and his responsibilities, you're fucked up in the head. #unapologetic

Not only was I dealing with emotional distress, but obviously, pregnancy uncontrollably affected my body. For instance:

A. Exhausted

Why? Because my body was trying to make a human, duh! According to the American Pregnancy Association, all those uncontrollable hormonal changes and producing more blood to carry nutrients to the baby caused this. Keyword = uncontrollable.

In other words, when your body is resting, that's when the body can focus on what's needed with minimal distractions.

If you think of your body as a machine, it can only function at 100%. If 90% of the body is focused on producing and developing a baby, then that only leaves 10% to do everything else, like fight infection, think, and remember stuff (i.e. pregnancy brain). It's pretty similar to a computer if you think about it. If turned off daily, it functions better rather than leaving it on all the time to maintain systems. If you don't, then eventually, the computer will begin to act up.

Rest is key. Not just during pregnancy but for your mental.

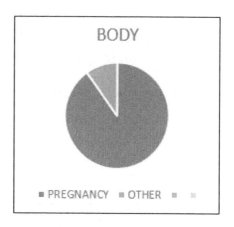

10% remaining doing:

- ✓ **Breathing normally**
- ✓ **Fighting disease**
- ✓ **Reflexes**
- ✓ **Give nutrients to mom-to-be like vitamin D and calcium**
- ✓ **Focus and cognition**
- ✓ **Digestion**

Essentially, your body doesn't give 2 fucks about you—only baby's development. You get what's left over only because you're housing the baby. Literally, your body is making you a "non-motherfucking factor", in my Evelyn Lozado voice from the show Basketball Wives.

Moving on....

Not only was I alone and pregnant, but my one-bedroom lease was coming to an end. So, I needed to find somewhere to live and kind of fast before I really blew up and couldn't do any packing. I had the option to stay in the apartment, but the customer service and the maintenance were both stressful. I had a leak in the same freaking place on the ceiling. Maintenance would come and "fix it" to make the ceiling white again, but a brown leak spot kept returning after a few weeks. A constant battle that a partner could've handled. I am convinced this was also why they say it takes 2, not only biologically to procreate baby but prepping for the baby as well. SMDH.

CHAPTER 16:

Remember when I talked about abandonment? Well, 2015 was the year people closest to me and that I knew the longest stopped fucking with me.

It started before I got pregnant in March.

In January of that year, Anthony came to town. Y'all remember Anthony, the Que who I've known since summer of 2008 Taste of Chicago.

Well, anyway, he came to Atlanta for work. Now I always felt a strong connection with him, and he always seemed to get me when everyone else thought I was mysterious or whatever.

After much deliberation about Anthony, Judas, and my life, I believed it was time to intentionally date. This was after Judas fed me BS about wanting a new job before a relationship. Blah blah. In my head, I knew he didn't want me long term with that response, but Anthony had literally always downright told me he was going to make me his wife. Since that's what I wanted, I was going to tell him in person, "We should," as he'd put it, "go ahead and make this thing official." And noooo, it was not because he was sloppy seconds to Judas or any nigga, but rather I really did want him and I to be together. Unfortunately, it just took me a minute to realize he was always what I wanted in a man.

So, when he told me he was in town, I went to go see him on a Sunday night after hopping off the plane from visiting family in Ohio. I prayed for the right words to say, the courage to say them, and for it to be received in the best possible way, even though I was like 99% sure he wasn't going to reject me. Then, like those romance novels and movies, we'd make sweet love all night long.

Where does the abandonment part come in? Just wait for it.

I pulled up at his hotel, where he was at the bar drinking and chalking it up with the bartender. We had a drink before he took me upstairs to his room. *This was the moment*, I thought to myself. I was going to tell him we should give this a go.

We got upstairs to his room, but I kept pushing his hands off of me so I could have a heart to heart.

Then all of a sudden, he got up from the bed to sit on the couch by the window. I was like *WTH just happened*, in my head. When I went to open my mouth to ask what just happened, he proceeded to say the following:

Anthony: "Ummmm... I don't think we should talk anymore."

My jaw dropped. Completely.

Me: "Excuse me?!"

Him: "I don't think you are into me, at least not how I'm into you. I mean, you wouldn't even let me touch you just now. And I've been chasing you since 2008."

Me: "Wow."

Him: "And I think you are too nice to say it."

Me: "Wow."

Now IDK about y'all... Correction: I know a lot of people would have gone off on a verbal rampage defending themselves, but that's not me. It could be a pride thing, but in my opinion, if someone tells me they don't want to talk to me anymore, I'm not going to beg them. Regardless of if my true intentions were to tell Anthony how much I did really like him and wanted to give us a real chance.

Instead, I gathered my belongings and left without a word. I had no words for someone who wanted to stop talking to me when I was going to tell him, "Let's do this."

I will say I held it together until I got in the car. Yes, I cried over this man. The man who had been in my life the longest and could see a future with. I think I was also upset with myself for not giving it a chance and not expressing to him that I did, in fact, want him.

So that was abandonment #1.

The following month in February of 2015, my birthday came around. Yass, Pisces season! Like Trap Beckham would say,

One time for the birthday bih
Two times for the birthday bih
Three times for the birthday bih
Fuck it up if it's your birthday bih

Ayeee!!!

But I digress...

I was trying to gather some friends for a birthday turn up, but since it wasn't a huge birthday year and I just got off the job market, I decided to have a mini house party. In addition to the birthday plans I had with Judas that he sponsored. Yes, I went back to Judas after Anthony rejected me. Ya girl had needs.

Naturally, who do you want to celebrate with? That's right, your friends. So I hit 'em all up to save the date-- the old and the new friends.

Some responded swiftly, whereas others didn't. I wasn't tripping though because some were new moms, some were traveling, and some were probably smashing boo. I totally got that people lived busy lives, but when I didn't hear back after a week, I sent a follow-up text just in case they got caught up and forgot to respond.

Crickets...

A few days went by, and I wanted an official headcount for food, drinks, and seating, so I texted yet again.

Me: "I know y'all are busy, but I'm getting a final count on who's coming... for those who didn't RSVP yet, let me know by today please."

A few declined, a few told me they no longer felt we had anything in common, and a few said they couldn't hang out with me anymore because I was a bad influence and partied too much.

I was literally in shock! I hadn't used the term *friendship* lightly since the 4th grade. To have *friends* whom I thought of as family want to break up, had me speechless. But y'all already know I was not begging anyone to be and remain in my life. Not bitter nor prideful, just not for me.

Needless to say, with abandonment #1 and then that, I had started to feel unwanted-- like that little girl insecurity tried to start burning its flames again.

I was sooo confused and NEVER saw that coming. It literally felt out of nowhere.

Abandonment #2.

And just in case you were wondering, no, my birthday was not the best. Thank you for asking.

At that point, interactions with Judas started to dwindle down because I wanted a real relationship and thought it was going to be with Anthony. But that was a no go.

On a positive note, I started my new job, and my co-workers seemed cool, so that was a plus. It's nice when your co-workers are also millennials. If y'all haven't experienced being the only millennial in the office, it's a real drag.

Another month went by, and it was Dave's birthday again.

IDK if y'all can recall, but that would have marked the 1-year anniversary of Judas and I meeting.

Admittingly, I was lonely and agreed to pregame with Judas and go to the party with him. To make a long story short, we pre-gamed per usual, and somehow, I got bent over the couch and felt his dick thrusting inside my apparently already wet pussy.

Yeah, I can't really justify what happened but...yeah.

Now 4 months later, here I was pregnant.... And by definition, abandoned #3.

I was uncontrollably in my feelings—at least when I could actually stay awake.

CHAPTER 17:

I'm sure you've imagined how you'd want and think these things ought to go. For me, it went a little something like this:

- You find out you're pregnant and freak out a bit
- Tell the father to be
- He's happy but also freaks out a bit
- You still comfort each other

Because Judas already had a daughter, I didn't think he'd react like this—especially with someone he spent so much time with. All the Father To Be had to do was cater to my pregnant needs and wants. Not too much to ask for considering it doesn't compare to actually being pregnant. But nope, I didn't get that.

Your friends and associates—the ones still standing—do the best they can, but they have their own lives to be concerned about. Plus, it wouldn't be the same as really being in it every moment of every single day. But they did their best. They checked in via text messages. They did what they could.

Then I got to thinking when I was like 9-12 years old, we had to move from Virginia Beach to Columbus, Ohio. I felt extremely alone. I didn't just feel it, but I was literally alone. I felt like I was in this jailhouse; my mom couldn't help me because she had severe MS; the church had only full-bred Koreans-- not like on the coast where much of us were mixed (basically the church in VA was not racist against me). And if we're being honest, y'all know black kids are the most judgmental group. IDK why since blacks came from an enslaved history. I didn't get it, but they weren't fucking with me because Halmoni was Korean. So, when I said I was alone, I literally meant *alone*. The point of this story down memory lane is because even at that age, with me being physically alone, I could feel God's love surrounding me.

So, this was how my brain worked:

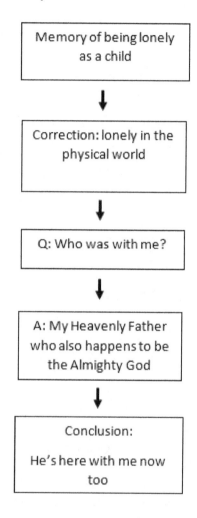

This is what I was constantly reminded; God was and still is my comfort.

Now, I understand some may feel like this came out of nowhere, but make no mistake, I have always had a special relationship with God. Even when I was a club rat circa 2007-2009 (maybe longer, I can't really say for sure lol), I always said a special prayer aloud before we got out of the car:

"Dear Heavenly Father,
Please allow us to be safe, have fun, and get in for free.
In Jesus name we pray, Amen!"

And so, it was done, and we were covered every single time.

Anyways, I stumbled across the Christian channel and started watching Joel Osteen and Joyce Meyers... like faithfully. Also, I would watch the series *The Bible*. You know, on those late nights when I was up nauseous. I would learn something new or be enlightened every single day. My spirit was really receiving what God was teaching me.

Each night I was in tears from feeling alone and abandoned. Then, I'd be in tears from the messages God was telling me via the TV shows.

Some of the things that God was telling baby and I were:

- The Power of Prayer:
    o I learned relatively early in life that prayer isn't a ritual, nor was there a wrong way to pray. I learned prayer is not some magic spell either.
    o Prayer is simply talking to God about the good, the bad, the ugly, and all in between.
    o The Bible mentions that with prayer and petition, it will be done.

"Do not be anxious about anything, but in every situation, by prayer and petition, with thanksgiving, present your requests to God. And

the peace of God, which transcends all understanding, will guard your hearts and your minds in Christ Jesus." Philippians 4:6-7

- o I had an epiphany that *"When two or three gather in my name, there I am with them." Matthew 18:20*
- o Now, it will always be at least 2 of us—baby and me.

- Our Words Have Power:
  - o I'm sure all of us, at some point in our earlier lives, had heard this, but you won't alter your words until it's truly received. At that point, you'll be held accountable for what you say. Take babies, for instance. You could tell them, "Noo don't touch that," but they'd go ahead and touch it anyways. Would you punish a baby who can't even speak and fully comprehend your words? No. This is because they don't comprehend the word "no" yet. Once they do and you tell them, "Don't touch that," then it's time to hold them accountable. They do that thing where they stare at you while touching the very thing you told them not to. You know what you have to do, right? Flick that hand real quick! They have to be punished.

When your mom tells you not to touch anything in the store

- The moral of the story was once you've comprehended something, then that's when you are held accountable for it. IDK about you, but I don't want to speak harm on my life, and then it come to fruition. No, thanks!
- Once I received that message, instead of saying, "I'm confused, depressed, lonely, and stressed," I switched it to, "Because words have power, I am not confused. I am equipped and happy." Even though it didn't come to fruition at that very moment, I still believed under the ocean of tears, it would be so.

Piggybacking off words having power, I started speaking life into baby. I was saying things like, "You are God's faithful, humble servant," and "You are blessed and highly favored." I always knew once I became a mom that my duty would be to teach. I had to be that example of what it means to be a Jesus Follower, and that moment started while baby was in the womb.

Confession time: In my thoughts, I kept playing the scene when Judas told me he wouldn't be there for us, and his intentional pettiness would be something I had to "deal with"—the complete opposite attitude I've ever received nor witnessed from him. It continued to baffle my mind and consume my thoughts, but I had to keep pushing through.

I was in tears so much every single night that I knew I could easily be a case for postpartum depression. As a result, I spoke against it! Remember clearly hearing Joyce say, "Talk back to the devil and talk aloud too; even if it made you look crazy." This was all because-- you guessed it-- our words have power. "I will NOT have postpartum depression! I will NOT be depressed, period! Get away from us Satan!" I would yell this out loud, all while the tears continued to stream down my face.

Believe it or not, every single time I'd say that, it would light a fire within me. And I'd feel better. Well, not better, but rather comforted to know our Almighty God (who happens to be our Heavenly Father) blessed us with the power of prayer and with our spoken words.

At that very moment, I had a light bulb go off!

"Even if Judas did not want to father, it would be ok because you are loved, protected for, and provided for by our Lord Jesus Christ." That is what I spoke aloud to baby, spoken to me by the Holy Spirit.

CHAPTER 18:

If you can recall, I'd watch *The Bible* almost daily to get my mind right. Each time I'd watch it, I'd hear my inner Holy Spirit teach me something different.

For instance, one night, I could repeatedly hear, "God is with me." Thus, I wasn't really as alone as it seemed, which also provided me with great comfort in between the meltdowns.

To keep it real, I wasn't perfect. I was human and had emotional breakdowns. However, I told myself I would never cry in front of baby once (s)he got out of the womb, and that I'd speak life onto us moving forward.

Anywho, by that point, I had *knowingly* been pregnant for a month; for a total of 14 weeks or so.

With this divine connection, I could hear more clearly.

Having said that, I believed God later revealed to me I was having a boy. So naturally, I told everyone that I was having a boy, and no, it hadn't been confirmed by the ultrasounds yet. However, I was still thoroughly convinced.

Not only was I convinced I was having a boy, but also:

1. God knows us more than we know ourselves. He knows what we can handle. A girl with all that attitude, emotion, accessories, and taking all my money—well, even *I* knew that wasn't something I could handle on my own. Uh uh, no thank you!
2. God has elevated my relationship with Him during the time of pregnancy. "My son" must be destined to do great things, and I was blessed enough to be his mother. HUGE responsibility that He thinks/knows I could handle it-- even when I was nervous as hell.

Once I felt like God revealed to me I was having a son, every day was like a broken record, I could hear God practically yelling, "Joshua! Joshua! Joshua! Joshua!" Two weeks later, I finally said, "Ok Lord, I get it, I will name him Joshua. Geesh." Lol.

Now, although I had ran and told anyone who asked that I was having a boy to the point I was saying "he" and "him" instead of "it" or "baby," I did not reveal that I was essentially instructed to name him Joshua. I did tell them I was contemplating names like Solomon, known in the Old Testament as King David's son and the wisest man ever lived; Noah, known in the Old Testament for obeying and being faithful to God to build the Ark; and Mason. And I *was* contemplating those names... as middle names, just not first names.

Ok, yes, I knew Mason was the odd non-biblical name, but I heard it once, and I liked it. *My* son, *my* name choice. Well, kinda-- middle name choice anyways.]

In case you're wondering, still no word from Judas. However, I did get notified by more than one person that he had been telling people, "I was just someone he helped around the house and fucked from time to time." SMDH.

I was beginning to accept that he wasn't going to be around but bashing my name in the streets and downplaying me like I wasn't shit... Uh uh! It would've been a bit different if only one person had mentioned it, but multiple people of different clicks came running to tell me; there must be some truth to it. So, I decided to send him a little text.

Me: "If you are telling people I was just someone you helped around the house, and that you fucked me from time to time, then please stop."

Him (30 seconds later...): "Who cares! It's not that serious! You're not that important. And don't text me again."

Me: "Why are you being so rude."

Him: "Get over yourself and stop texting me."

Another round of tears hit me like a random summer storm, except I had all the reasons to be in tears.

I just didn't respond. What could anyone say to that? It would've just got my blood pressure up on top of everything else. I couldn't do that to my baby nor myself. Correction: I tried to keep my cool because everything I did would stream onto the baby.

.

.

.

A few days later, it was finally time to know the sex of the baby. Officially. I was still 100% confident that he was a boy, and I was to name him Joshua. No, still no one knew just yet.

[Sidenote: Did I tell y'all that Halmoni would always say, "You better hurry up, get a husband, and have my great-grandson."? I guess she was over the girls; with my mom and then me.

Never mind the fact I wasn't married. She'd always call to vent about how Judas could just leave and not care, and then say maybe he'll come around all in the same breath. She was all over the place too.]

Anyways, it was the day. I couldn't believe I had made it this far. Halfway. Omg!

I got into the ultrasound room. The Tech put the ultrasound gel on my huge belly and showed me his hands, his head, and his little legs kicking. He just kept kicking that ultrasound tool until he finally opened his legs to show us his little wee-wee! Ha! I knew it! See!

Now everyone who thought I was being crazy or picky about what I wanted will see; don't play with me when I tell you God revealed something to me. ... but for real.

I had the Tech email me the photos for proof.

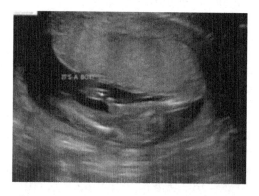

Other than knowing this was the photo the Tech gave me as proof I was having a boy, don't ask me what exactly is showing there. I don't see a human in those things. Lol.

Nonetheless, I was soooo, soooo, so happy!

The confirmation that God has been with me and comforting me was amazing.

Amongst all the bliss, I still had to get to work. Buzzkill, I know. I was an hourly employee, so I needed all the money I could get.

I will say my co-workers were truly a blessing at that time. They made work fun, tended to my needs, and made me feel cherished. I mean, I was at work 5 days a week for 9 hours per day. God placed them in my life at the perfect time, doing the perfect job.

So, when I told them that it was officially confirmed I was having a boy, they were so excited for me too! IDK why, but a new baby filled everyone with euphoria.

Well the workday FINALLY ended so when I got in the car, I called my grandparents:

Ring! Ring!

Ring! Ring!

Ring! Ring!

Like 4 or more times.... You know how grandparents are—they "can't hear the phone" or "the phone is broken".

Grandparents (simultaneously): "Hello? Hello?"

Me: "I went to the doctor today."

Them: "What they say? Is everything good?"

Me: "They did the ultrasound to see if it's a boy or a girl."

Halmoni (like an impatient toddler): "What is it?!? What is it?!?"

Me: "A boy."

Daddy (What I call my grandpa): "Aye! Alright now!"

Halmoni starts screaming in excitement in the background, and I could hear her telling my mom's nurse that I was having a boy. She FINALLY came back to the phone like 2 minutes later.

Halmoni: "What are you going to name him? Joshua?"

I'm going to let that sink in for a moment.

Yes, y'all. Of all the names in the world, and she said Joshua! I did not tell ANYONE! It was soo crazy!!

Me: "Yeah, how'd you know?!?"

Halmoni: "I like that name..."

Daddy: "Yeah, Joshua. Joshua is gonna be my nigga."

Me: "What?!?"

Halmoni: "Don't say that!"

Daddy started laughing in the background.

Halmoni: "Ok, you going home now?"

Me: "Yeah."

Halmoni: "Ok, get off the phone while you're driving."

She didn't know that I put the phone on speaker and tucked it inside my bra so I wouldn't have to physically hold it, but whatever.

Me: "Ok, bye."

Halmoni (singing in the background): "It's a boy, it's a boy!"

Meanwhile, I was practically yelling at her to hang up the phone. They always forget that step for whatever reason.

Click~

SMDH.

Now, for real, how did she know??

Further proof from the Lord that my son is to be called Joshua-- not my choice, His choice. He has chosen my son. How special was that?

Those were the moments you'd want to share with the other "parent." Even though Judas still hadn't reached out to me, nor responded to any of my texts asking why he was treating me like his enemy, I still wanted to do the right thing by telling him he was having a son. Maybe, just maybe, he'd soften up and want to step up as he should. As a *father* should. Also, the Bible says to kill with kindness.

6/1/2015-

Me: "Hey"

Crickets.

Hours later... still crickets

Me: "I got some ultrasound photos today. Would you like to see them?"

1 minute later...

Him: "No, I'm good."

I don't even know how to describe how I felt. It was like my heart rapidly sank to the floor. He didn't even want to see ultrasound photos of his own son.

You know what, though? I sent one anyway. The one showing "it's a boy" typed on it.

Can't nobody say I didn't try—not Judas, not Joshua, and not my spirit!

I had no words. Seriously. Well, no nice ones anyways that wouldn't get me extremely rattled up, causing my blood pressure to spike and affecting Joshua's too. Remember, it was not just me anymore. Literally, my body was being shared, or rather Joshua was taking over.

Soooo... that obviously didn't go as foreseen in my head whatsoever.

"I cannot make this shit up people," in my Kevin Hart voice.

It made no sense to me either. None! My brain was buggin' over this. Seriously buggin'.

I didn't deserve the treatment Judas was giving me. Everything I did for him when we were talking, and now, I was the mother of his son. I should be on a pedestal just for being his son's mother. Right or wrong?

AND...

Remember how Judas and I would speak about babies and how "our kids would be cute with curly hair?" His words y'all, not mine. I remember telling him how I wanted a son, and he said, "I gotchu." Welp.. there it is. No, this wasn't planned, but when you're talking to someone, eventually babies do come up. Also, HE brought up babies to me, not the other way around. Go figure.

I mean, it's not like I ever slashed his tires, made a drive-by, had my gay friend show up at his job dressed in drag causing a scene, nor had glitter delivered in the mail so that shit would get all over the place... for days. (All ideas presented to me by my friends, that I turned down btw.) I didn't do anything... except keep this baby. My son.

I told Joshua he better not EVER treat a woman the way Judas was treating me, especially the woman of his kids, which I hope would be his wife. I said," You better be a good God-fearing respectful man," as I rubbed my belly.

CHAPTER 19:

Some may have thought it was too soon, but I was a planner and absolutely hated to rush at the last minute. Plus, if I got any bigger, I was not going to do anything extra. Correction: *when* I got bigger. Ugh.

What am I talking about?

The baby registry. Yes, it was time to hit up Babies R' Us. I figured I could tackle that early on a Saturday morning and go get some Mexican afterward. Yum, a burrito bowl.

Anyways...

Yes, baby registry time. I can't even lie-- I did get emotional on the drive there but kept telling myself that I would be alright. That *we* would be ok.

I got in there, filled out paperwork, and waited on someone to be available. That was like 30 minutes of my life, but it felt like FOREVER, though. They did end up telling me my insurance covered a breast pump, which was super helpful!

I finally got the scan gun thingy and hit up the aisles. It was suggested to start at the strollers and go clockwise until I returned to the service desk. And that list they provided me was sooo lengthy.

I figured it wasn't going to be too bad. But I was so wrong. So very wrong! I had noooo idea baby stuff was so freaking expensive. On top of that, why were there so many options???

I took a few deep breaths and scanned for the 2-in-1 stroller-- you know with the car seat combo. I liked combos. I liked the 2-in-1s overall. A highchair. Beep!

- Bedding... *ok, pick a theme. One that had an entire matching set available. ..beep!*
- Clothes- *Aww, look at these preemie onesies. Too cute... but I doubt he'd need that since I feel like he's huge already.... Let's see, ok:*
  - Newborn..beep!
  - 3mo.. beep!
  - 6mo... beep!
  - 9mo... beep!

(Yes, I told y'all I was a planner.)

Beep!

All that other stuff like the tub and bottles were stressful. Like why were there sooo many different kinds? Why couldn't there had been like a maximum of 3 options.? Tubs that were jacuzzi style, with a swing, with or without a drain hole. WTF?!?

AND don't get me started on those bottles and nipples! Curved bottles, bottles without all the measuring lines, long bottles, short bottles. THEN came the different nipple flow sizes. I had noo idea those existed! Slow flow or faster flow. Ugh, no one explained this to me! I was mad at myself because, apparently, I was supposed to research all that stuff beforehand.

Each aisle became more stressful to the point I just wanted to sat down somewhere. My feet were killing me! Then 3 hours later, I was STARVING! I just wanted to give up. Then I got emotional when I saw couples trying to figure it out together; meanwhile, I was there by my damn self. That nigga Judas wasn't a first-time father, so when I harped on it, it just pissed me off even more. I just wanted to go buy a bottled water and sit on those rocking recliners... so, I did. Omg. *Heaven*, I thought to myself.

As I was sitting there, I was like, *I need one of these.* So, I looked down at the price tag and thought, *"Nope, I don't need it that bad."* I only rented an apartment that I needed to find movers for next week. Ugh, the to-do list was getting longer and longer, and all I wanted to do was rest.

With me moving into a 2-bedroom, I'd have room for the recliner, but that would cost extra to hire someone to deliver it.

At the time, I had no extra funds. Although I did start to save the little that I could—and I do mean L-I-T-T-L-E—there wasn't anything more I could do, unfortunately.

I FINALLY managed to wrap that registry up. I was literally praising God that shit was over. I was EXHAUSTED! So much so, that I couldn't even stand in line at the Mexican restaurant to order my burrito bowl. I was forced to hit the drive-thru and order a large! #unashamed #unapologetically

.

.

.

Something told me it would be cheaper to rent from a homeowner rather than via a complex. So, I was on the hunt. I already gave my wretched apartment complex a notice that I was up out of there. Then they had the nerve to ask me why. Ummmm, could it be because they refused to permanently resolve the leaky ceiling instead of just painting it as a cover-up? I think, yes.

Anyways, I looked at some places up the street, and I settled on a 2-bedroom, 2-story townhouse for only $200 more than what I was spending in that 1-bedroom apartment. Granite countertops were more my style anyway.

Now for the moving part. U-G-H!

I had to pack up by myself. I told people I was moving, but do you think anyone volunteered to help? Nope. I had to flat out ask people.

One friend named Charlotte did end up coming to assist me. She was so helpful. Char helped me find some extremely affordable movers, AND she went with me to get the moving truck as well. Once the movers arrived, she had me sitting down. I was so exhausted. And then Natalie helped me unpack. So, Char was the one there in the beginning, and Natalie arrived later. They both helped me unpack and put my Sleep Number back together.

I did not have to lift a finger, but I did have to pack by myself. Lots of standing. Lots of bending. It sucked, but who else was going to do it? No one. Hard truth was that I HAD to move.

As you can imagine, I did absolutely nothing that Sunday. Too tired.

.

.

.

Remember I told y'all that some friends cut me off earlier in the year? That was devastating for me. For whatever reason, something (or God) told me to text them to let them know I was expecting Joshua on 1/1/2016. So, I did. Surprisingly, they responded with, "Congratulations." So that was that.

.

.

.

The next day, I got called into the office of our HR Director and my Supervisor. I was nervous like I was a kid being called into the principal's office.

HR: "So I wanted to speak with you about something and asked Reyna to join us."

Reyna was my direct supervisor.

Me: "Ok, am I in trouble?"

They both busted out laughing.

HR: "No, nothing like that. We wanted to offer you a permanent position with us. And I apologize this took so long, we had to wait on the budget approval."

Me: "Really?!? That makes so sooo happy! Thank you!"

HR: "You've been such an asset for us, and we are pleased to officially bring you on board. Do you verbally accept?"

Supervisor: "Yes, you've been wonderful to work with."

Me: "I cannot believe this. Wow, I'm speechless.... Yes, I accept!"

Supervisor: "You've always spoken up in meetings, came up with great ideas that we are currently implementing, professional, our entire HR teams loves you. The Project Management Team adores you as well since you've been working with them on those special projects. They, and we, appreciate and notice your talents. So, we want to design a position specifically for you (once it's approved in a few weeks) that involves streamlining processes and working with PMs to implement and execute. You'll basically be a part of the Workforce Management Team collaborating with PMs, HR, Marketing and I.T."

HR: "Plus, this would be a good opportunity for you and Joshua to have- the insurance and at least double the salary for you both."

Me: "OMG, I think I'm even more in shock. Thank you so much!"

Hugs went all around as I thanked them again and let them know how much it meant to me. The Supervisor walked out, and Dave, the HR Director, kept me in his office.

No, no! Nothing like that. Gross! I was pregnant with another man's baby, and he was married with a family of his own. PLUS, I had spent time with his wife and 2-year-old daughter on multiple occasions. They were generous enough to gift me with some baby gear, like the baby swing. Dave was such a blessing for me personally and professionally.

Anyways, he wanted to tell me that his wife, Leah, was having another baby! I hugged him again and immediately texted Leah to congratulate her. So exciting!

That was the best Monday I had ever had. A permanent position and then after a few weeks be promoted with double the salary.

Ladies and gentlemen, that was called God's favor... 100%!

That Friday came along, and my co-workers had set up a baby shower for me. IKR. They were so sweet. My handsome, gay co-worker set up the event, and you know it looked up to par—from the bite-size cupcakes, the hydrangea flowers, to the décor. Flawless. He was definitely showing off his event planning skills, and I was so grateful he volunteered his services for me. You know how you don't really expect much from work events, but I could tell everyone was excited about it and generally cared for me.

They cared so much that the Executive team gifted me the car seat I wanted. Just in case you were unaware, car seats are not cheap. Each of the Staffing Coordinator team members bought me a present. The bedsheets, bibs, clothes, and stuff I actually needed. Bottles too. Not just too many sets of the same ole clothes.

[Sidenote: I specifically told everyone to not buy me ANYTHING with monkeys for the obvious reasons. I was having a black son, so with American History and "modern" America, my son will not be compared to any freaking monkey.

Many researchers have revealed in articles like the Coon Caricature: Blacks as Monkeys, of the *"hateful association between Blacks and monkeys or apes was yet another way that the antebellum South justified slavery. Blacks were considered by some Whites to be more simian than human, and therefore had no self-evident rights, including freedom. After the Civil War, the emancipation of slaves, and passage of the 13th, 14th, and 15 amendments to the Constitution, White bigots used the association to justify Jim Crow laws, and the use of violence, such as the lynching of Blacks who challenged or threatened the status quo. The general acceptance of the evolutionary theories of Charles Darwin was easily twisted into a means of identifying further "evidence" of the primitive status of Blacks.... the result of a lifetime of conditioning via the long history of stereotyped anti-Black imagery that depicts Blacks as less than human."]*

Anyways, my co-workers made me feel extremely happy. I knew that was favor from the Lord; our Heavenly Father was providing for us (me and baby Joshua).

I was truly blessed.

CHAPTER 20:

You may or may not be wondering what I was doing besides work, sleep, and getting my Jesus on. Well, not much outside of that actually. Lol.

You may ask or wonder about the guys I was talking to. Well, they were still there.

Yes, y'all, still there! And they knew I was pregnant too!

Some were guys I met online that were essentially text buddies—pre-Joshua. Once I found out I was pregnant, I started to ignore them. I just felt weird entertaining niggas that were not the father.

There was this one guy I had to just flat out tell him, like, "Dude, I am pregnant, so you should probably stop texting me." He *still* continued to text. The check on me kind of texts. Now THAT I was okay with. Eventually, I ended up ignoring those too.

Basically, I fell off the planet. Then I was feeling depressed that I didn't take pregnancy photos. Why didn't I? Because they cost money that I didn't have to just hand out all willy nilly. Plus, this didn't seem like a joyous occasion-- single mom from 8 weeks pregnant. Terrible.

Then God told me I could take a free selfie to show off the belly, so I'd at least have 1 photo. So, me, Joshua, and my recent Dominican blowout took a bathroom pic selfie... I thought it turned out cute outside of the toilet paper photo bombing it.

_jenuine

I said, "Fuck it, I won't be ashamed of being a single mom ... ever!"

I know what it's like for a parent to be ashamed of you, and I don't want that for Joshua. I posted that selfie and the "it's a boy" ultrasound photo on social media. After I posted, I got hit up in my DM, had comments, AND texts. Some of those messages included "Congrats!" while others said, "Is this a joke?", "Is that his penis?" and stupid shit like that.

One of my personal messages was from Chris. (Y'all remember the guy serving in the Navy with the best head of my life and that curved dick? Mm, yeah, him.) Well, he congratulated me and checked on me pretty regularly after that.

But then...

Well, you know you've heard those stories of pregnant women being super horny as hell, like to an entirely different level? This moment started for me. So... I sexted the fuck out of Chris while he was overseas. I felt weird about it, but at the same time, we were not really going to have sex. He was in Bahrain. I was not going to fuck a nigga with another man's baby in my belly. It was too much to think about. Now the sexting part I could do... and well. He would send me dick pics, and it would bring back the most wonderful mind-blowing memories. I mean, I remember this one time when it was so orgasmic that my leg would not stop quivering for hours. Y'all, it was uncontrollable! Like a dog getting his belly rubbed, and the leg would just keep going and going and going like the energizer bunny. Ooooo shit, yep. This was how that nigga had me.

On another note, not only were the sexual hormones sky rocketing, my patience had plummeted. Like a record low.

The landlord I had was uber annoying! Omg! And don't get me started on the maintenance guys. These men were both inconsiderate, unprofessional, and just plain stupid.

The landlord would constantly text me when I was trying to sleep, and I couldn't figure out why. He was on Bill Pay for the rent. Leave me the fuck alone! Then he was always trying to stop by and "check on things." Leave me the fuck alone! I just ended up ignoring him.

Then there were maintenance issues with the same damn toilet. So, the Landlord gave his maintenance guys my number, and they'd always try to come over at times I was unavailable, then had the nerve to show up late. Eventually, I had to cut them off and demand for new professionals. I even had to yell at them and tell them I was pregnant. Either they were going to fix the shit permanently and on my time, or I was going to task it with someone else and file complaints. One guy told me to find someone else and that I was unreasonable. Nigga bye!

Ugh!!!!

Then on top of that, I couldn't get comfortable to sleep anymore. So, I was even more pissy.

But then...

Omg.. y'all are going to think I am making this shit up...

I walked into the kitchen one night to get something to drink. I turned the light on, opened the refrigerator doors, and saw a lizard crawl into the fridge. Yes! You read that correctly. A freaking lizard, gecko, thing! I screamed and shut the door. I freaked out on what to do for a good 10 minutes or so. Then I heard the neighbors shut their door. Okay, should I go ask them for help? Yes! I walked over there with my headscarf on, and the 11-year-old daughter answered the door. It was just the mom and daughter. I explained I had a nasty ass lizard/gecko, and it had crawled into the fridge. The mom was like, "Yeah, we have those all the time," like that shit was fucking normal. Just in case y'all didn't know, THAT SHIT WAS NOT FUCKING NORMAL! It was NEVER okay for wildlife to get inside the house!

She went on to say her daughter would keep them as pets for a while and release them. WTF! That was not sanitary. Nonetheless, she could tell I was freaking out. I'm talking like 10 out of 10 freak out. So, she and the daughter came over and caught the damn thing. I was so grateful and relieved!!!!

They left with the gecko thing, and I washed the fuck out of my hands, put gloves on, and tossed all the food in the trash from the refrigerator. I cleaned the fridge, sanitized it, the floors, and the counters. EVERYTHING!

Once I got to the front door, I saw a crack at the bottom. That was probably how that fucker got in. I took a photo to send to that fucking annoying ass landlord and told him about the lizard. His response, "A lizard? Are you sure?" That dumb fucker. *Yes, I was sure you dumb fuck!*

From that point, I was paranoid as shit! Then it took FOREVER to have a maintenance and pest guy come to treat and fix that issue. I complained daily and told the landlord that it was causing stress for the baby and me. His response was, "I just don't understand how a lizard got into the house." *Me fucking either but come seal this shit up! Ugh!* After 2 full weeks on his nonsense and dumb ass comments, someone finally came to seal the shit up. How I survived? Only Jesus. Seriously.

CHAPTER 21:

Of course, I had to call my grandparents every day. Not so much because I missed them, but because I needed to make sure they were doing what they were supposed to. You know, things like eating their vegetables, taking their meds, etc. Plus, they worried about me without a husband and all.

I told Halmoni about my co-workers having the baby shower and the gifts I received. She was thrilled. Then, she told me to find a crib. "Not a cheap one either, a safe sturdy one." Correction: she demanded I go find a crib like now. I planned to have him sleep in a bassinette until he got big enough or when funds were available for all that, whichever came first. She, of course, wasn't having it. She basically bullied me into purchasing one online, and she paid for it.

Now IDK about y'all, but I wasn't big on online shopping. Photos didn't really do justice. I needed to feel the product; HOWEVER, I did purchase it with her credit card because she graciously offered... BUT I needed it like now. I couldn't wait 3 more weeks for delivery and installation. So, I opted for pickup in the store.

Click... submit!

Shortly after I fell asleep, I kept tossing and turning. I could not get comfortable for nothing, and I had like 7 pillows in my king size bed-- propping me up here, there, and in between. Ugh!

So, I laid there listening to classical music for Joshua's brain activity. I could have played those on the piano, but the piano was at my parents' house. So, I found a classical music station to stream from my phone. Songs like:

- Chopin: Nocturne Op 9 No 2
- Mozart: Symphony No 40 in G Minor

- Beethoven: Fur Elise

Yes, all that. I believe classical music improves brain health.

"It ain't cute to be dumb," as I told Joshua. It was essential, especially for a boy of color.

Then when there was a super active song, like:

- Bach Toccata from Toccata in D Minor or
- Beethoven's Symphony No 5 or
- Rimsky Korsakov Flight of the Bumblebee

I had to turn the station. Those were too hype for late nights. It was time to be calm. Yes, I was training Joshua early to calm the fuck down at night. I did not want Joshua to be nocturnal. After all, I was going to be a full time working single mother.

I had to think about all that kind of stuff.

So, like I said, when those "hype" songs came on, I turned to the Christian station called Air1. They played poppy Christian music—cute head boppers and toe-tappers. Since my job as a mother was to teach, welp there you go. Joshua would know and love Jesus from the womb until forevermore in paradise. "You better," I said to him. Lol, but seriously.

I looked at my phone, and it was already 4:00 a.m. My mind went wondering about Judas again. Not like having wet dreams or hoping we'd be in a relationship, but rather hurt and confused. He could have been in this with me. Instead, he chose not to be a part of our lives. *Why* I kept asking myself. In the midst of my tears... yet again... I fell asleep.

Moments later, I heard those darn birds chirping. Then 5 minutes later that freaking alarm! I was so annoyed. Eer!

I naturally hit the snooze button and laid there for the 8-9 minutes it allotted me before it went off again. I got up, got ready, and headed to work. On my way to work, I received a text. I wondered who could've been up texting me this early. Was it Judas?

Once I got to a stoplight, I looked at my phone. I couldn't believe my eyes...

It was one of my old friends that cut me off earlier in the year. Yea, I couldn't believe it either.

I couldn't read the entire text because well... I was driving. I was driving and pregnant at that... so I was being extra cautious.

Once I did get the chance to read the texts, it was an apology and a makeup text.

With the abandonment I had received, everything happened for a reason, and I guess she was also reappearing in my life for a reason too.

After some thought, I realized I valued her as a person, and it meant something when someone acknowledged, apologized, and then wanted to move forward, together. As a result, I got a friend back. Yay!

Soon after, bestie came over with her SUV and drove us to Babies R Us for J's crib and toddler rail attachments. It didn't occur to me, but it was suggested to buy the rails at the same time. Apparently, it was typical for newer models to come out within a year, and those rails would not be made available for purchase when it would be time to transform the crib into a toddler bed. I'm glad I took his advice because he was right in the end.

Once we got it, I couldn't bring the crib inside nor upstairs. Luckily, there were some neighbors outside to assist.

Bestie stayed, and we gave each other a rundown on our current lives. She didn't really know Judas that well because she wasn't in the Meetup group. She was busy being a wife and mom OTP (outside the perimeter). Lol.

We ended up putting the crib together. Well, okay, *she* put it together. I wasn't much help because sitting there and bending over was challenging. It hurt, and I felt like I couldn't breathe, which made sense because Joshua was taking ALL the space. It was the convertible kind with the drawers and changing table attached.

.

.

.

Since there was a spirit of reconciliation in the air (yes from days ago), I thought I should text Judas to extend the olive branch yet again.... THEN I had to let it go.

September 27th, 2015:

Me: "Eventually we are going to have to discuss this. I refuse to believe that THIS is the same person that told me he was *in like* with me, revealed his goals, the one who lit up when he spoke about his daughter, the one I've prayed for, the one who said he loved and appreciated me, and the one I thought I knew and spent so much time with. We can't continue this disconnect and/or bad blood especially with a son arriving soon. It doesn't make sense. So let me know your availability so we can talk."

No reply.

.

.

.

September 29th, 2015:

Me: "Happy birthday btw."

No reply.

.

.

.

October 18th, 2015:

Me: "I'm sorry you feel the way you do. Moving forward please don't expect much from us."

No reply.

.

.

.

No one can ever say I didn't try for Joshua.

CHAPTER 22:

When Monday rolled around, I had another doctor's appointment to check on our progress. When I got there, the front desk lady told me I had a balance. That took me by surprise because I had been approved for pregnancy Medicaid by the state.

Me: "I've never paid a balance before because I have Medicaid."

Her: "We don't accept Medicaid."

Me: "Since when? That was the insurance card I showed from my first appointment months ago. And again, I've never been presented with a balance nor ever paid a co-pay if that were the case."

Her: "Ma'am, we don't accept Medicaid."

Me: "So why didn't you say that when I was a new patient months ago and every time I've visited since then?"

Her: "I don't know who helped you in the past, but we don't accept Medicaid."

Me: "Please go look in my patient file because I'm not going to argue with you. I am pregnant."

She slammed the glass door, and I could hear her complaining to the doctor that I had Medicaid. Meanwhile, he told her to go look in my file and see what was copied. *The same exact shit I told her ass.* And y'all already know I stood there waiting.

This was oh so frustrating. I was not a new patient, I had been there several times before that day, and this was ultimately taking time away from my coins. She finally opened the door to say, "You can take a seat and we will get back with you," then slammed the door again. At that point, I was beyond livid, so I knocked on that door to

165

confront that unprofessional bitch. I knocked, and I knocked. No answer. I knocked a third time and said I can see someone behind the glass. Then that bitch finally opened it, and I told her I wanted to speak with her manager. Some guy in the background told her to open the door and let me talk inside so there wouldn't be a scene in the waiting room in front of the other patients.

I walked back there and explained to the doctor how rude and unprofessional his staff was. Not to mention, why would they accept me as a new patient if they were now claiming they didn't accept Medicaid. Why wasn't this shared from the beginning? Who in their right mind would visit a doctor that was not in-network with their insurance? I had been there more than once, so this made no sense! If it were true that this office didn't accept Medicaid, where the fuck were the invoices for the balance I had allegedly owed?

The doctor told me he would have the office manager take a look when she returned later in the week. We went ahead and proceeded with the check-up. I mentioned I wasn't paying for anything, and they need to contact Medicaid for payments.

My checkup went fine, btw.

Leaving there, I was still so heated. By the time I left, I was starving. So, I HAD to stop and get food, or I would have died. IJS. The entire thing had me wanting to cry, and then the fact I had to deal with that nonsense solo made it worse. Still, I held the tears back. I couldn't go into work looking puffy in the eyes.

After I got settled into work, I got a group text. It was basically reminding me that my baby shower with my friends was coming up on Saturday. This one girl, who was a newer friend, offered to throw one for me. So sweet of her. Thanks girl!

Since I was trying to cut costs down—also because I was just grateful people wanted to have a baby shower for Joshua and me—I said we could just have it at my house and do a pot-luck style.

For the rest of the week, my phone was blowing up about this baby shower. I needed help moving some furniture around, so I asked who'd be there to help setup. No one really spoke up, but Octavia said she'd try to arrive a little earlier since she had an event in the morning. See, she had started her own graphic design business called Creative Juice in Atlanta (check them out online). So, with her creative eye, I wasn't worried about the details like I normally could have been.

Now y'all remember, I was a planner and didn't like to procrastinate and wait on others. So just in case no one brought any good food, alcoholic beverages, or photo props, I went on and came up with a plan to make beef and chicken kabobs with cilantro jalapeno dipping sauce, this blue cocktail I found online to match the color theme, jello shots as welcome shots of course, and put the photo props on the tableclothed table. I can hear some of y'all saying, "You doing too much," but I just felt the need to do something, especially when again, people were willing to celebrate Joshua. Celebration is what I needed too. So, I just did all that the night before; I marinated the meat, made the sauce, and set the tequila jello shots in the refrigerator.

The morning of Saturday, October 24th, 2015, came around, and I waited to text people to see if they were still coming and bringing what they said they'd bring. I started to panic because the shower was scheduled for 1:00 p.m. and it was already 11:00 a.m. As a result, I kinda started moving the little things out of the living room. Because I was moving at a pregnancy rate, I realized that it took me like an hour. Nonetheless, I got it done. I made the blue cocktail, checked to make sure the jello shots had set, and took a "quick" shower. Don't worry, I did not taste the drinks-- I just smell tested them to make sure they were strong enough. They smelled about right.

I put on this tight dress to show off the bump and put those kabobs in the oven. Shortly after, the doorbell started to ring. Guests were finally arriving, but at that point, I was exhausted. I just unlocked the door and sat down somewhere. Then I noticed my feet were swelling. *Great*, I said to myself. I mean, I *was* on my feet all morning, so it did make sense. As a result, I propped my feet up while we ate and mingled before the games and gifts.

We played the classic games.

The one I haven't heard of was actually tasting the baby food and guessing what it could be—gross. I did not partake.

The girls did come through with the gifts, and I was grateful because IDK if it's obvious by now, but Judas had gotten nothing for Joshua. I even had 2 friends collaborate and buy the stroller and car seat combo. In all seriousness, between the baby shower with my co-workers and with my friends, I literally did not have to buy anything except diapers and wipes. God did that! He really did. And I was (and still am) so grateful. Shoutout to you all for that-- spies and all! #slightshade #foreshadowing

Anywho, people started to leave around 8:00 p.m. Yes, they were there all day, and I was beat. Before they left, I had goodie bags for them to take home... condoms and a shot of tequila. Yes, I did send everyone home with a condom. It was the responsible thing to do, or they'd be next. IJS!

Shanelle was the last one out around 9:00 p.m. Once she left, I went to urinate (for the umpteenth time that day, I might add) and realized as I was washing my hands that I wanted to take a selfie to remember this day. Even though the girls took photos on their phones, who knew when I'd receive them. So, I relied on myself.

As I was taking the selfie, I felt something drip down my legs. In my mind, I was like, *I didn't just pee on myself because I literally just went.* Unfortunately, it could happen when you're pregnant. Then my mind went to, I know my *water didn't just break, I only just hit 30 weeks today!*

I looked down.

Oh no! Oh no!

It was blood!

Yes, blood! (Devil showed up #1.)

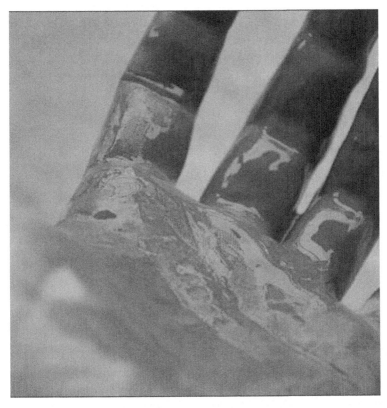

I didn't have any pain, but even though I wasn't a certified medical professional, I knew *this* wasn't normal.

I called Shanelle to come back and take me to the hospital. I also left a voicemail for the doctor.

Something (or Jesus) told me to go upstairs and gather some pants, a towel for Shanelle's car since I was bleeding out at an alarming rate, my contact case and glasses, and phone charger—all before any pain developed.

I still didn't feel any pain, but I rolled like 15 sheets of thick observant paper towels and put it in between my legs so the blood wouldn't stain the carpets. I couldn't, nor did I want to pay for that.

About 15 minutes later, Shanelle arrived in a panic. I told her I wasn't feeling pain yet, but we should still hurry. I got to the car and put the towel on her seat. She was flabbergasted, but I didn't want blood stains in her car. I mean, how could that be removed?!?

Still no pain.

We drove, and about 2 exits from the hospital there the pain came. And it was ferocious!!!!

Normally I would have tried to hold my composure, but this pain was... umm way too much! I had to scream, and I literally couldn't move.

From that point, she ran like 2 red lights, and we pulled in front of the ER.

The security guy could tell I was in distress and got a wheelchair, even though he said he wasn't supposed to leave his post. (God showed up #1.)

It took me a minute to even get in that wheelchair because it was extremely painful. But he helped me and wheeled me to the front desk while Shanelle quickly parked somewhere. Probably illegally... but this was a true emergency!

I got wheeled to the front desk, and the lady who just got checked in took one look at me and said, "She can go before me. She's pregnant and bleeding a lot!" (God showed up #2.)

Then the bitch at the front desk went, "Well, I have to finish checking you in because the system can't save my work, or I'll have to start all over."

Yes, y'all; again, I cannot make this shit up.

I literally could not speak at that point. *Bitch, don't you see I'm pregnant... and bleeding here!!!!!* I yelled in my head. (Devil showed up #2.)

Shanelle rushed in, unknowingly to my rescue. (God showed up #3.)

Basically, she yelled at that cunt, asking for my insurance card while I was still bleeding profusely and still wasn't able to speak.

From that point, it all began to slow down. Like, everything went into slow motion.

Nurses came out for the other lady, but the lady let me take her place. After some back and forth, the nurses finally agreed to it. Why they were even going back and forth about it, IDK.

They put me in the hospital bed, gave me an IV, and it was obvious they were in a panic about the blood. Why would said medical professionals be in a panic? Again, IDK. They finally hooked me up to machines and searched and searched for a heartbeat.... Nothing.

I heard one of the two nurses say under her breath, "Where is he?"

The other nurse went, "What's his name?"

I thought I said, "Joshua," but evidently, I didn't base on the nurse's response, "She's unresponsive."

It was obvious to me they were trying to get my mind off this situation, but it wasn't going to work.

Then the nurses were whispering, "I think she is having a miscarriage."

I immediately looked at Shanelle and actually heard myself say, "Nooo!" as my eyes started to tear up.

It sounds weird or unbelievable, but I could see the darkness in the left corner smirking. As if the devil had won. (Devil showed up #3.)

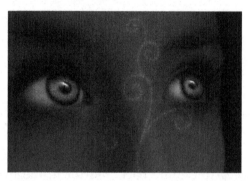

Even though I could feel my eyes getting watery, no tear ran down my face. At the same moment, with the darkness over there smirking his ass off, I prayed and heard God commanding an angel to rescue us. Literally within 5 seconds, a random black female doctor just so happened to walk by and asked if we (the nurses) needed some help.

Unknown Black Female Doctor (UBFD): "Hey, I'm a surgeon assisting tonight's shift. I was walking by and heard some commotion. Do you all need help in here?"

Nurses: "Yes! We can't find the baby's heartbeat," they replied in desperation.

UBFD: "Well, we can tell there's a baby, so let's find him," she said calmly.

How did she know it was a boy? I thought to myself.

UBFD touched my arm, and at that instant, I heard a voice say, "It's going to be alright. God sent me."

Then there it was...

Thump.............. thump.................. thump...

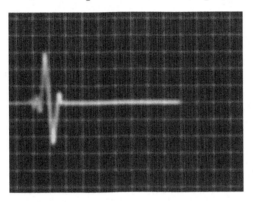

It was extremely slow, and we could barely hear it, BUT it was still there!

The relief and comfort that instantly filled me.

I could see Satan turn from the pitch-black darkness to a gray cloud in confusion.

UBFD: "Ok, we need to do an emergency C-section with anesthesia. Send her off, stat!"

Glory be to God and praise Him for saving us, I said in my head since I physically wasn't able to speak.

(God showed up #4, 5, 6, and 7!)

In the midst of my praise and gratitude, a man (I guess the anesthesiologist) tried to put the mask on me. I pushed it off of my face. The man was not paying any attention and was blocking my nostrils. Like, it started right underneath my nose and went down to my chin instead of putting it on top of my nose and mouth area, correctly. I thought, *Ain't no way in hell after all this, was I going to die of suffocation from this careless anesthesiologist.* (Devil showed up #4.)

The anesthesiologist finally realized why I was pushing the mask off, apologized in his Caribbean accent, and placed it on me properly. The next second, I was out like a light.

CHAPTER 23:

I opened my eyes with the clock staring at me. I was able to see it said 7:40 a.m. before my eyes uncontrollably shut.

I opened my eyes with the clock still staring at me. This time I was able to see it said 3:00 p.m. and heard the girls chatter before my eyes uncontrollably shut again. Even though my eyes were shut, I could still hear them chatting.

Moments later, I heard Char slightly shouting at Natalie. Telling her that she needed to get the fuck out and wasn't welcomed here because Natalie was a backstabber for calling Judas last night. Meanwhile, Natalie was trying to justify that she should've called Judas because "it was the right thing to do". Blah blah. Since my eyes refused to open and I had no voice. In my mind, I was yelling at that bitch too. Essentially, I was saying the same exact things Char was saying- as if she was my voice when I couldn't speak.

After Char put Natalie in her place, I heard the chatter again, but like white noise. Then I really dozed off but not before my heart melted from my friendships within that room.

Did you not know that darn clock was staring at me, yet again when I opened my eyes? However, this time, the nurse was there, and my body allowed me to speak. "When was Joshua born?"

Night Nurse: "Well, hello! He was born Saturday, 10/24 at 10:24 p.m."

Me: "Where is he? Can I see hi....m?"

Night Nurse: "He's in the NICU, and they are taking good care of him. No, not yet, you need to get better first."

My eyes shut off again, but it was weird because I could still hear.

I heard Karen talking shortly after that. I guess they were already acquainted. Karen was an outgoing HR attorney and a friend. The Night Nurse told Karen I had woken up asking about the baby and that I had "shut down" in mid-sentence. She also said that it was normal since I was in recovery from "the heavy trauma." It is amazing that her and Joshua are still alive."

Then I heard Karen calling Halmoni, telling them I had woke up briefly. It was on speaker. Halmoni was talking about, "Hallelujah, and thanks for calling."

I wondered how Karen got their number. *Maybe someone gave it to her? Or she somehow got into my password-protected phone,* I said to myself.

Then I dozed off... yet again.

The next time I woke up, I saw it was 9 something in the morning, and the Day Nurse (DN) was there.

She told me it was a miracle we were alive and gave me the rundown:

- Joshua was in the NICU and needed a blood transfusion that morning. He was doing fine and responded well to it.
- Both of us lost a ton of blood due to the placenta detachment.
- They would monitor me to see if I needed a blood transfusion as well.
- I had a C-section, so I was stitched up under the bikini line. "The surgeon did a great job, actually," she said. Because I cared about that—insert sarcasm here.
- Since it was an emergency C-section, the pain was more excruciating because they were not delicate with my organs compared to a planned surgery.

- It was going to hurt to move at first, but I had to get up and start moving again for my own sake and circulation.
- The past few days they put air compression wraps around my calves and feet since I didn't move at all and needed help with circulation.

DN: "Can you try to sit up now?"

Me: "Ouch, ouch! No."

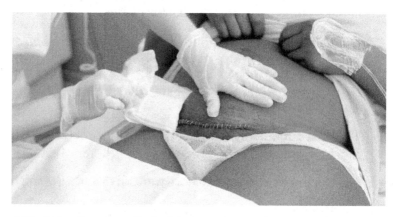

DN: "It's ok. Try a little bit at a time. The NICU will not allow you to see your son until you're able to stand on your own or at least be able to walk to this wheelchair I've set beside your bed. This is your first goal."

Then my eyes shut again. But that was a record so far of keeping them open!

All said in my head again, *OK, my goal is to see my son. I MUST get up and get to that wheelchair. That won't be too difficult…. Lord, help me get to that chair!*

I snoozed off again.

That uncontrollable falling asleep thing was pissing me off. I had shit to do! Like see Joshua! Ugh!

I finally woke up again and remembered what the nurse told me. Last time, I literally could not lift up whatsoever. This time through the pain, I lifted up like a centimeter. I didn't push too hard because I didn't want the stitches to burst. No need for another emergency, but I was grateful that I had Medicaid to pay for all this. Otherwise, I would just have to leave. Period. Real talk.

Anyway, I kept what they called pulsing every 15 minutes until my body uncontrollably shut down. Each time, I kept lifting higher and higher. So, I was making progress.

Let me just say this: you don't realize what muscles you regularly use until that muscle refuses to be used. My abs were like dead weight at that point. I kept pushing through though. The goal of a mother... the *strength* of a mother.

12 hours had gone by, and I could finally sit up. Well, mostly sit up. I basically begged the night nurse to wheel me to the NICU to see Joshua. She told me I had to get up 3 more times, and then she would. Luckily a couple of minutes before midnight struck, she agreed to wheel me, my IV, and catheter to the NICU. Victory! Well kind of. The pain was excruciating, but I was anxious to see Joshua. I didn't want him to think I had abandoned him like Judas had.

We got on the elevator, and that little bump on and off hurt like a motherfucker. I was secretly praying my eyes wouldn't shut on me. The moment I could FINALLY lay eyes on my baby boy. 2 days later. 2 days stronger.

When the NICU room opened, all I heard was the beeping. *Beep... beep... beep...* as I rolled through.

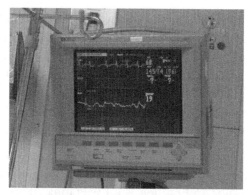

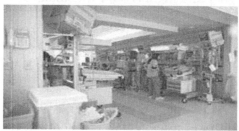

There were so many incubators. I was staring at each one until I found him—lying in the middle incubator, snuggled up with a massively huge diaper because he was so tiny, and with tubes going in all directions. I got as close as the wheelchair could allow it and attempted to stand. I quickly realized that was too ambitious. I painfully sat back down in the wheelchair and placed my hand inside the incubator.

I said, "Hey baby, it's Oh-Ma" (Mom in Korean). I had already told him while he was in the womb that he'd be trilingual, so he had already become familiar with me referring to myself as Oh-Ma.

When I said that, he opened his little eyes, and looked at me looking at him. Then, he closed his eyes again.

It was love at first sight. All the emotional and mental pain from Judas, and now this physical pain was all worth it. I had more than enough motivation to keep my body moving because I was all Joshua had in this physical world. God lit a fire in me and reminded me I was now a mother.

It was simply beautiful.

However, only if I had gotten the heads up on what was about to come. Whew man! No comparison.

Pain does not and could not describe what happened after I laid eyes on Joshua. Unfortunately, this was only the beginning of our journey.

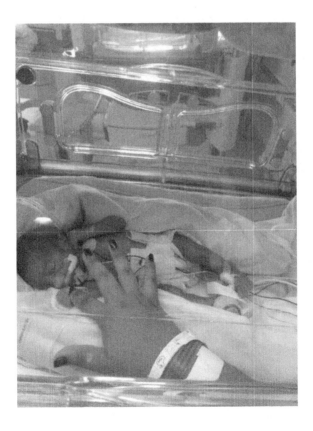

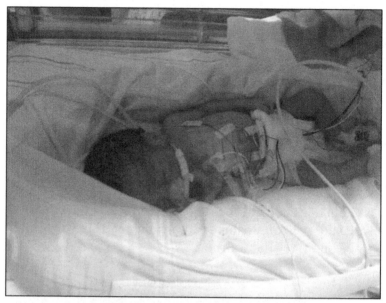

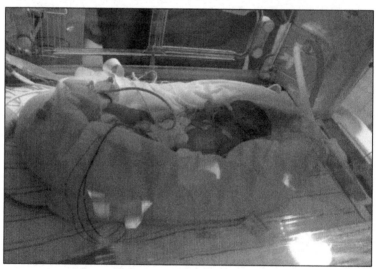

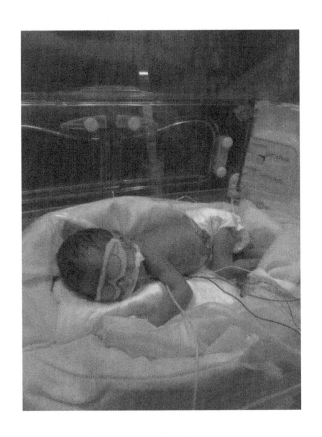

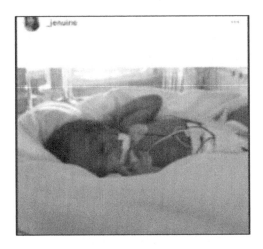

Look for Part 2

You Don't Know My Story, Perseverance

Coming soon..

Made in the USA
Middletown, DE
17 April 2020